THE WARRIOR

Moving from Misery to Victory

HEATHER R. ELIZABETH FOWLER

WESTBOW
PRESS®
A DIVISION OF THOMAS NELSON
& ZONDERVAN

WestBow Press books may be ordered through booksellers or by contacting:

WestBow Press
A Division of Thomas Nelson & Zondervan
1663 Liberty Drive
Bloomington, IN 47403
www.westbowpress.com
1 (866) 928-1240

ISBN: 978-1-9736-3083-8 (sc)
ISBN: 978-1-9736-3084-5 (e)

Library of Congress Control Number: 2018906929

Print information available on the last page.

WestBow Press rev. date: 6/29/2018

To all past, present and future warriors

TABLE OF CONTENTS

ACKNOWLEDGMENTS

First, I need to acknowledge my gratitude to my Heavenly Dad who sat with me as I typed every one of the words that fill these 192 pages. I felt the calling to write a book years ago, but whenever I came up with an idea for a book, it went nowhere. After "Chicago", the book was given to me as a whole outline. I knew, at that moment, that this is the project for which my Savior had prepared me. To say that this book wouldn't be here without Him is a gross understatement. This book is a gift from Him.

There have been several editors who have guided me as this dream became a reality. The first people outside my family to read this book were the content editors: Cathy Flores, Gail McDaniels, Pastor Yvonne McCoy, and Pastor Luke McKinnon. My chief editor, who looked for every misplaced comma and misunderstood sentence, is Cory Schweitzer. Thank you all for your help.

To the ladies who will always be my boots on the ground; you Warrior Women are my inspiration. I have seen many of these first warriors fight to find, and then work through, their David Moment. After doing so, I have seen the Creator of the Universe breathe life into dry bones. Not only did you ladies go through this Bible study, and, in some cases, the retreat, you poured life and truth into other women's lives. This has been the privilege of a lifetime. Thank you, Sherri Bailey (always my right hand), Stacey Harris (if Sherri is my right hand, you are my left), Tandi Paez, Loretta Vega, Jennifer White, Briana Baumann, Rachel Bynum, Loryn Phillips, Stephanie Vega, Ashley Banks, and Penny Bakke.

I wanted this book to have a military theme. I have never been in the military, but thankfully, there are people close to me who have. Thank you Lee Trussell, Steve Lee, Tom Romero, and my anonymous contributor. The sacrifice you have given to this country can never be properly and completely conveyed.

I also need to thank my family. They not only endured "Chicago," they have heard about it and dissected it with me over and over again for years. My husband, Alan, has been with me when I cried, reliving portions of the last few years, all over again. He has read and edited every word multiple times – even when it meant looking at it after he was finished with his work late at night. I love you dearly, and am so blessed to call you my God-given partner in life.

My daughter, McKenzie, has been my biggest cheerleader (and I have had some amazing cheerleaders). Much of her college career has been spent dealing with, first this event, and then the book. Through this process, sweetie, you have become my editor, sister warrior, and friend. I love you! (And yes, you taught me not to add exclamation marks everywhere, but this time it was warranted.)

I think my parents, Jotina and Lee Trussell, have sold many copies of this book before it even came out. They have told all of their friends about it, and in the process, been an amazing witness to the power of Jesus. My mom has been to every event I've hosted with Warrior Women. Mom, you were my very first best friend. Thank you for your never-ending love, friendship, and encouragement. My dad became my chief military advisor. Dad, no matter what I needed, you provided. This book will always have your fingerprint upon it. I am the person I am today, because you have always showed me what strength and sacrifice looks like.

My two spiritual daughters, Stephanie and Loretta, have contributed both ideas and content. Thank you, ladies, for your love and help throughout this process. I have been witness, through the writing of this book, to the power of the Living God, and the work He has done, and continues to do in your lives. Thank you for being open to the prodding of the Holy Spirit, and for the love you both have poured out onto me.

Finally, thank you my sweet son, Collin, for allowing me to write his story for The Warrior. Throughout your lifetime, you have shown me what the power of God looks like in the life of someone who loves Him. You have trusted Him enough to bounce back from every setback you have ever experienced. I know you are a member of the army of the Living God. He is teaching you and guiding you down a path that none of us truly understand yet, but we both know that He is preparing you for a role that will use these experiences powerfully in His plan. Stand back, God is doing something with and through you, that will be amazing to witness, and I am blessed to have a front row seat. Not only did you inspire this book, you inspire me daily.

Dear Warriors,

I'm overjoyed that you will be joining us on this journey. Oftentimes, when you join a Bible study you work through large chunks of Scripture, but this study will be a little different. Instead of studying a book of the Bible, we will spend seven weeks looking at just one chapter of one book: Psalm three.

This chapter was written by King David after his son, Absalom, conspires against him in order to turn Israel against the king and assume the throne. At the beginning of Psalm three, King David is hidden, alone, hurt, and in fear for his life. Throughout this study, we will refer to this moment as a David Moment.

This chapter works through a range of King David's emotions; from despondent and afraid, to reassuring and explorative, to victorious and forgiving. We will slowly and methodically join King David on his journey of trust in who God is, and the faith we can have in Him.

You will choose a moment or season in your own life that was difficult; a moment that possibly even made your faith wobble. Each week, we will take a magnifying glass to this rich portion of Scripture, to glean from it the things we can do in our own life, and in our own David Moments, to take us from afraid to victorious. Even though you may work through this study with a group of ladies, this study is between you and your Savior. If, while in the midst of the study, a new David Moment occurs, work with it. Change your David Moment, or add it to what you are working with already.

Finally, I ask that you prayerfully choose to open up and truly join this study. The homework can be long. There are three lessons each week given as homework; altogether, those three lessons will take approximately four hours to complete. Divide up the work as you see fit, but finish. We are zooming into this study so deeply that missing a week of homework can mean you miss an important part of what you need for this puzzle. Furthermore, the subject matter can open up wounds that were in the process of healing, but cover yourself in prayer and stick with it. Psalm three is an amazing chapter in the Bible that teaches us how to use those difficult moments in our lives to overcome them, bring glory to God, and win the battle as the warrior that God created you to be.

I love you and am praying for you, as you become *The Warrior.*
In His love,
Heather

Introduction
What Are We Fighting?

My sweet sisters in Christ, how I hope this study helps you! My first desire during this study is for you to start identifying yourself as a warrior. I want you to see that we are in an amazing position to fight, because we know that the war itself is won. Praise God! What war, you might ask? You might not realize it, but there is a war being waged all around us; it started the second Satan wanted to be considered equal to our Father in Heaven. Ever since that moment, Satan has been fighting for influence both in this world, and in your heart. It is a war between good and evil, but also so much more. Whether or not you choose to fight, you are a warrior in the greatest war ever fought. The second Jesus took a breath in His burial tomb, the war itself was won, but there are still battles to be fought. That is where we warriors come into play. Our General is unequalled. He is omnipresent, omnipotent, and omniscient; He is everywhere, all-powerful, and knows everything. He wants a relationship with us so that He can teach us how to win our battles, and bring peace to us and glory to Him. The most amazing part of your identity in Him is that you are His beloved. He has the ability to help a praying mother in Kenya, a refugee in Syria, a man who lost his job in Germany, and your crisis all at the same time. He loves and adores you.

My second goal is for you to learn how to gain the courage to fight. My prayer is that through this study, you will be able to identify and dissect what I call your *"David Moment."* This is a situation that keeps nagging on your heart, destroying your motivation, and eating away at your courage in life. We will learn about our own struggles as we watch what King David went through and how he dealt with it, to bring glory to God and find victory in his battle. It is that moment or situation that overwhelms you to the point of knocking your faith off balance.

In the first lesson, I will share my own David Moment with you. This study is designed to help you learn to overcome your David Moment. You will discover that God has already given you the ability to formulate a plan to trust God in, and through, that situation. Furthermore, God can use your struggle to springboard your once wobbly footing to a battle plan that will proclaim God's victory! The first step is to pick up this study and choose to follow it to the end. Congratulations--you've taken the first step. Beware: it might be an unpleasant journey at times. Reliving difficult times in life can be grueling. With trust in our Heavenly Father, we can pick up our swords, discover what we are fighting, come up with a battle plan, and proclaim victory! I'm excited to have you join me as, together, we learn how to fight our battles and celebrate victory in the war that is already won!

During Week One, we will simply work to identify what we are fighting. We will break down the large items into their core issues, as well as uncover the hidden battles we are fighting within ourselves. Finally, we will uncover our real enemy, and realize that he is already defeated! Let's get started.

Lesson One: Discovering your David Moment
Lesson Two: Six Core Hurts We Battle
Lesson Three: Who Are We Fighting?

Lesson One
Discovering your David Moment

The bags had been unpacked from what turned out to be our horrifying trip to Chicago; a friend was on her way over with dinner, my teenage son, Collin, and his big sister, McKenzie, were on the couch watching a movie, and my husband was in his office catching up on emails. That's when the gravity of the previous three days finally hit me. I am the strong Mama Bear who can withstand anything. I will make everything okay. I will be a pillar of strength. I will set a good example of trust in God so that my kids aren't afraid. At that moment, when all the jobs I had to do had been done, I sat alone in my room and was utterly empty. I didn't cry; I was devoid of emotion. My faith was wavering. I felt like an Olympic gymnast on the balance beam who has lost her footing, arms flailing, legs kicking out to the side, and a desperate determination to right the situation. Only today, I couldn't "right" the situation. I was at the mercy of a God whom I felt was nowhere near me. I was hurt, disappointed, bewildered, and afraid.

It had all started when Collin was in the second grade, and his computer teacher came to my classroom (I taught at the same school) to tell me that she was worried about Collin. Collin loved computer class and excelled in it. The teacher told me that Collin couldn't remember how to turn on the computer. This was big. For him, turning on the computer would have been just as easy as saying hello. I followed her to Collin's class; when I got there, he looked at me with eyes half open and a sweet smile on his face. "Hi mom!" He seemed very tired. Our family was familiar with seizures, and we knew they could look different than the typical seizure you see on TV, so we called the doctor. We got in fairly quickly to get an EEG. When the results came back, our worst fears were realized. Collin was having seizures. With millions of questions starting to form, and anxiety and panic bubbling up, I stopped and closed my eyes. I knew that God has always been my Shepherd, and would take care of me and lead us all through this. At that moment, a supernatural peace poured over me like honey coating a sore throat. I thought this was going to be a twig in the road; something we noticed, but was hardly a problem. It would be over before we knew it. I was wrong.

For the next six years, we searched for the right doctor and the right "cocktail" of medicine. The first doctor prescribed him medicine that was so strong it was like drinking water from a fire hose. The medicine got rid of the seizures, but also put thirty pounds on his eight-year-old frame. In three short months, he went from a small, scrawny kid to a child teased for being "chubby." It wasn't long after that, that we searched for a doctor who would take a different road with us. We found her. She was willing to do what it took to get him off that medicine and find him a better one. It took another five years to find the right cocktail of medicines, but we did. However, in those five years he had countless *Absence Seizures*. I became the expert in the house at spotting his seizures, which was a trick. They simply made it look like he was sleepy; he didn't fall, he didn't turn blue, and he didn't shake. Every time he had a seizure we went through the same routine. I would ask Collin if he felt funny and he would say no; he couldn't tell he was seizing until he was seventeen years old. Knowing he was having one, I would ask someone else in the house that I knew couldn't see them, in order to talk myself out of the reality of the situation. Once I was ready to accept the truth, which was only moments later, we would take action to stop the seizures and call the doctor. Our doctor would change the cocktail of neurological medication, and we would start over.

Starting over entailed a sort of realignment with my conversation with God. Every time, the conversation went something like this, "Why God? I will accept that the answer to my prayer could be, 'not yet.' I'm ok with that. Is it time now? Was this the last problem?" As of December 2015, we had found our cocktail. Collin hadn't had a problem in a long time. Was he cured now? It was these emotions, as well as our hopes and prayers, which made the events of that December trip to Chicago so difficult.

We had planned a short family trip to Chicago after Christmas. Our most precious moments are those spent with the four of us together as a family. We are all too aware of how our life is about to change with two soon-to-be grown kids: grown-up jobs, spouses, and families of their own. We only had four days, but it would be four days spent the way we love it: the four of us, laughing, eating, and playing together.

All of that came to a screeching halt when Collin started throwing up the night before we were to come home. You have to understand that vomiting, especially at night, is a major seizure trigger. We knew we had to hurry. We took him to the hospital, got him into a room, and tried to get the vomiting to stop. Each time he threw up, we reset our internal clocks. "Maybe now it's over," we kept telling ourselves. We were in a furious race to stop something we had no control over. I felt like I was running for my life while being required to stand still. Thoughts raced through my mind. "Collin needs anti-nausea meds. He needs to take his regular meds, but we have to do it when he won't throw them up. We have to get this to stop so that he can get the eight hours of sleep he needs."

Finally, it had been an hour since his last time getting sick so we took him back to the hotel where he could sleep. I stayed up the rest of the night watching him, as if that alone might stop anything bad from happening.

We let Collin sleep as long as possible. A fleeting thought said, "Stay here," but I ignored it. All I kept thinking was, "Get home. Get home. Get home." So we quietly threw things in bags, and at the last minute, we got Collin in the car and headed toward the airport. As we were on our way to the gate, I thought I saw what I didn't want to see: an Absence Seizure. So I went through my normal routine. Collin denied feeling weird, and my sweet hubby, trying to talk himself out of what he was seeing as much as me, said everything was fine. When we got to the gate I found a seat for me and my daughter. My husband went to get some coffee, and we laid Collin at our feet to go to sleep. The next moment changed everything.

I heard a noise and looked down—Collin was seizing. Not the sleepy kind; the terrifying kind. Seeing your child go through something horrible doesn't get any easier, simply because he's been battling it his whole life. Each time is new, horrific, and desperately upsetting.

The next ten minutes felt like I was the star in a movie with special effects like *The Matrix*. Everything happened quickly, but in slow motion at the same time. I looked at McKenzie and said, "Get Dad!" She ran off! I knelt down to take care of Collin. He was exposed. People were staring. All I could think of was to cover him so that when he woke up, he would have his dignity. I looked up to see McKenzie crying and praying over the phone with her best friend. I looked at a man who was next to me staring at my son. I don't judge him; I think he too was traumatized at what he was witnessing. Most people go through their whole life not seeing someone seize. It's scary. While on my knees next to my son, I looked back at the man and said, "Get help!" When I turned back around, there were two people kneeling next to my son explaining that they were doctors. They did their "doctor thing", helping my sweet son. Next to me was a very quiet lady who held my hand, kept asking if I was okay, and tried to take care of me. Within moments my husband, Alan, and the EMTs arrived and started hooking Collin up to machines. Before we knew it, Collin was on a gurney on the tarmac and on his way to the second hospital within twelve hours.

The next hour was a wildly busy time. We had to convince the EMTs to go against protocol and allow me and my daughter to go with Collin in the ambulance. Alan realized that our gift cards we had been using for meals were in our luggage on a plane bound for Albuquerque. The kind people from the airline allowed Alan to search through a mountain of luggage to retrieve ours. Alan had to find a rental car during a busy holiday weekend in Chicago; he then had to locate the hospital where we were taken (which required calling the hospitals in the area because no one told him where they were taking us). We booked the very last seat on the last flight in from Albuquerque that night for Collin's girlfriend, so that we could make a last ditch effort at making New Year's Eve fun. I called his regular neurologist to get answers to the questions swirling in my head. We called family about what had happened, the change in plans, and to get their help in prayer. We spent twelve hours in the hospital, and Collin was released. The next two days were spent ignoring the fact that this ugly event ever occurred. We had fun, played games, ate great food, and made New Year's fabulous. My mind never had a chance to stop until I was in my bedroom at home, with everything done. I felt hollow, empty, and utterly alone. My husband is my rock, my best friend, my lifetime love, and my emotional cornerstone, but it is my Savior and Lord who fills me and, for the first time, I didn't feel Him there.

I tried to pray but couldn't. I tried to cry but couldn't. I tried to emotionally connect with what had just happened, but I couldn't. My feeling of emptiness transformed into feelings of hurt and anger. It is difficult to admit that emotion. As a Christian, and especially as a ministry leader, you aren't supposed to be upset at God, but I was. I truly believed God would heal my son. Why hadn't He? This continued for a couple of days, until God reached into my nothingness and grabbed hold of me. I started remembering times in my life when God had been working powerfully in my life. God had never allowed me to go through something difficult alone. Why would this be any different? It was at that moment that I felt God wrap me in His arms and made me feel safe, reliving "Chicago" through His eyes. With the most love and compassion I have ever felt, God held me and wrapped His love around me so tightly that I felt safe reliving this horrible time.

God showed me, step by step, that He had been there the whole time. He showed me the blessing in this occurring at the end of the trip. He gave us three days of love and laughter as a family before this happened. When we took Collin to the hospital the first time, where was it? It was across the street from the hotel. The hospital was literally twenty feet from the hotel door. When we were at the hospital, waiting to be admitted, and the staff has to decide where on the list to put you to get a room in the ER, what happened? Collin fainted with the insertion of the IV, and got a room immediately. At the airport, two doctors instantly showed up at my son's side to help, and God even sent a sweet soul to comfort me. Suddenly, I started seeing the situation so differently. God had foreseen all of this, and did things to help. He was there! Then God sweetly, kindly, and compassionately, led me to the realization that we could have stayed at the hotel; I was the one who chose to go home. The Loving Creator of the Universe who spoke light into the world and who had the grace to send His son to die for me, also held my hand during one of the most difficult times in my life. He was there THE WHOLE TIME! It was never me who would withstand anything. It was never me who would make everything okay. It was never me who would be a pillar of strength. It was never me who would keep my kids from being afraid. It was Him! It was my Abba, Father! It was the Creator! It was the Alpha and Omega! It was the one who has given strength to the powerless and defeated evil! It was my gracious Heavenly Daddy!

That was my "David Moment." King David's moment occurred in a hiding place (many believe it to be a cave) when he was overwhelmed, scared, and bewildered. In Psalm three, David writes of being scared for his life while hiding from the people of Israel. His son had ultimately betrayed him when he turned Israel against David. All of Israel was hunting King David in order to kill him. David wrote about what was happening--what people were saying, his fear, what God had done for him, his peace in God's plan, the renewal in his desire to fight, and ultimately, his forgiveness of those who were hunting him. He wrote the entire psalm while in the midst of the problem, while people were still trying to kill him. I believe we all have a "David Moment" in our lives. When these moments happen, you have two choices: stay a bewildered, wilting flower, or stand with God and fight. David chose to fight.

I look back on my David Moment now and realize that it was at that instant, in the arms of Christ, that I became a Warrior. I was ready to accept God's timing in healing my son. I was ready to fight my worry and fear. I was ready to fight for the courage to pursue my purpose in life. I was ready to fight with Christ as my shield, in whatever battle He chooses for me to fight.

We've all had a David Moment. It is that moment when you aren't quite sure how, or even if, you are ready to take the next step. The first step to becoming a warrior is finding out **what you are fighting**. For some of us, our David Moment is obvious. It looks at us every morning in the mirror, it is in a child's good morning kiss, and on the pillow at night. For others, it may be that there is a time in your life that is filled with these moments, and your David Moment is really a David Season. Still others may feel they haven't had a dramatic time in their life that fulfills this definition. Wherever you are, I ask that you prayerfully allow today's study to help you discover the Moment, or Season, that you will use to dig through this study. Let's do this together, and use that moment to uncover the warrior within you.

King David Connection:

In order to discover your own David Moment, we have to delve into David's life and see what led to his feelings of devastation and hopelessness. David suffered a huge loss when he discovered that, for four years, his son had been plotting against him to overthrow his leadership and become king. David was dealing with his emotional pain while hiding in a cave, afraid for his life. I can't imagine his sorrow.

Let's read the account of the conspiracy of David's Son, Absalom, in 2 Samuel 15:1-12:
How did Absalom conspire against his father?

_____

_____

Did the people of Israel know the whole situation?

_____

Personal opinion: Do you think the people of Israel, who were tricked in the conspiracy, held any responsibility for what transpired? Why or why not? The Bible does not give us an answer to this question, so this is a personal opinion question.

_____

_____

_____

Of course, David was devastated. Read 2 Samuel 15:30 and put how he was feeling into your own words.

_____

_____

_____

While hiding in the cave, alone, hopeless, and devastated, David started his conversation with God in Psalm 3:1. What was David's first concern?

_____

Yes, he had enemies but had God provided friends and helpers?

_____

Personal reflection question: Isn't it true that when things go wrong in our lives, everything seems bleak? It is often difficult, while we are in the midst of turmoil, to see how God is taking care of us. Has this ever happened to you? Did you look back at the situation and see God in the middle of that situation holding your hand? Tell us about it.

_____

_____

_____

_____

_____

How can we start finding God during our troubles today?

_____

_____

_____

_____

Thoughts in the Foxhole:

A foxhole is a small hole fitting one or two soldiers to provide shelter against enemy fire. It is also a place where soldiers stop and think. During battle, there is so much moment-to-moment thought involved in the fighting, that you rarely have a chance to think about anything except what is at hand. When a soldier gets in his foxhole, everything stops for a time. In a foxhole you feel safe, maybe for the first time in days, and your mind has the opportunity to wander. It wanders back home to what your family is doing, it wonders to your friends in battle, it wanders to how you got here and if you'll make it out alive. I want your foxhole to be a safe space for your mind to wander. I have specific things that I am going to ask you to think and pray about while you are in your foxhole. So get somewhere safe, quiet, and alone, and wrap yourself in God's loving arms. It's time.

Sweet sister in Christ, I want you to pray for God's peace, His loving arms, and His grace. When you feel safe and prepared in Christ, I want you to ask God about the David Moment He wants you to focus on during this study. I know that, for some, this is going to be difficult. God is there! Allow your Abba Father to love you through this. I believe that if you allow Him to, He will immediately start working on your heart, giving you the courage, determination, and motivation to start fighting. The first step in the battle is discovering what you are fighting.

I want you to think back to a moment, or a situation, that hasn't or doesn't seem to leave you. This could be a traumatic event that occurred in your past, a difficult situation you can't seem to work though, or something you face day-in and day-out that requires courage. Take your time, pray, and ask God to reveal what He wants you to uncover, so that He can give you the tools to fight.

I'm giving you the space below to think through possible David Moments in your past. You will have the opportunity later to decide on one specific moment. For now, brainstorm. Remember, your David Moment is a time or event in your life that emulates the first moments of Psalm 3 (vs 1-2) when David's faith wobbled. He felt desperately alone, uncared for, and afraid. Your David Moment will fulfill similar feelings in your heart. This won't be an easy process. There could be several moments for some, and others might have difficulty finding any. This space is designed to allow your mind to wander, so do just that. I believe we often tend to cover over problems like a partially made bed. The bedspread on top looks nice and neat, the pillows decorate the bed, making it an inviting place to sit, but when you take the pillows off and pull the bedspread down at night your bed is still a wrinkly mess underneath. So whip the pillows and bedspread off the bed and let's get down to business. I promise, our loving Heavenly Father is on the other side of the bed helping you.

_____

_____

_____

_____

_____

_____

_____

_____

_____

_____

LESSON TWO
SIX CORE HURTS WE BATTLE

Thank you for sticking with this study. I'm proud of you! For some, the previous lesson made you relive one of the most difficult moments in your life. Did you feel our Heavenly Dad wrap His arms around you? Reliving my David Moment was the most powerful motivator I have ever received. I love thinking about the fact that the same God who said, "Let there be light," and slew David's giant, also loves me enough to compassionately and patiently sit next to me while I hurt. God's love is enveloping and motivating, but it is also very powerful! It is powerful enough to teach us how to become Warriors.

During my journey with this study, my husband has shared his David Moment with me. I feel so honored that he has allowed me to share it with you.

"My David Moment started 'cooking' in March 2007. This is the month that the financial crises in the Mortgage Industry started. We knew that some of the big companies were going to have trouble, but we thought we would dodge the bullet. My father, sister, and I started our family company with integrity as a goal. We have always thought of ourselves as the "Bailey Building & Loan" of Albuquerque (from *It's a Wonderful Life*). Our company, and family, goal was to help people experience the American dream. We had always made good loans to good people and worked with people when trouble hit them. In October 2008, we realized we wouldn't dodge the bullet. A number of factors collided in one month to make us realize that our family-run company that had survived thirty years of market ups and downs would not survive this crisis. I took it on myself to keep the company afloat long enough to sell what we could of the company and get a retirement for my father. I worked 12-16 hour days calling in every favor I had earned as a leader in the industry. I spoke on mortgage banking all over the world and had many powerful friends. Surely someone could help. I called people, I scrambled to make portions of our business worth selling, and I tried to reassure worried employees.

In short, I was desperate to make everything OK: for my father, for my sister, and for my employees. I had to sell our company, and it was the worst possible time in the history of the mortgage industry to sell. Everyone wanted to get out of the industry, not buy another piece of it.

Then, on February 23, 2009, my hope plummeted. I sat in my office with the realization that I was not going to be able to save the company. If our little company had days left, I would be surprised, because at that moment, it looked like there were only hours. For the first time since childhood I shut the door to my office, turned up the music I was listening to, put my head on my desk and cried. I felt like I had run a marathon with a bear chasing me. I was at the end of myself. I don't even remember driving home, but I remember my wife's smiling face when she opened the garage door to see me sitting in the car. I didn't know what to say. I didn't know how to tell my best friend that all was lost. When I lumbered out of the car, my wife grabbed me, wrapped me in her arms and told me everything would be Ok. 'The company is done, I have failed. In all my work to save the company I didn't make a contingency plan for us. I don't think I am going to have a job tomorrow. I won't be able to pay tuition for the kids and I won't be able to make our house payment. I'm so sorry.' Without dropping her smile, or her hug, my wife looked me in the eyes and said, 'Nothing matters other than our faith and our family. The kids will go to public school and we can move into my parent's house. It will be a big adventure.' It was. God grabbed my hand and walked my family through the toughest season of my life."[1]

Our David Moments can all be whittled down to six basic hurts. I know that's hard to believe, but think about it. When you strip all of the onion layers away from your David Moment, there is a basic hurt that needs to be discovered. When that hurt is unmasked, it becomes easier to pray over and deal with the root of the problem. Here are the basic hurts:

1. Fear
2. Anxiety/Worry
3. Disappointment
4. Loss
5. Pain (physical, emotional or spiritual)
6. Temptation

As you will see, many, if not all six, hurts can fit your David Moment. For Alan, all six fit to some degree, but he has learned that it was anxiety/worry that fits his situation best.

I know you are starting to digest the idea of where your David Moment fits, but don't worry about that yet. Let's look into David's moment.

The King David Connection:

Let's read about the moments after David hears about Absalom's betrayal. Read 2 Samuel 15:13-30. What was happening in verses 13-29?

_____

_____

_____

I can totally see myself in what David was doing. When he got the news of the betrayal, he knew he had to move fast. He had to escape. There were so many details to be handled, that he didn't have the time to think about or deal with his hurt. When everything settled down and he'd had a chance to think, what was his response (found in verse 30)?

_____

_____

Can you relate to David? He finally has a moment to let the heaviness of the situation sit on top of him. Look again at 2 Samuel 15:30. God takes time to describe David's appearance. Describe what David looked like.

_____

_____

Why do you think he had his head covered and was barefoot? Read Ezekiel 24:15-18 and Esther 6:12. In what situation did people cover their heads?

_____

No matter the core issue, many of our hurts can seem like mourning. What was David mourning?

_____

_____

David went further than the head covering; he also removed his shoes. What could this have been symbolic for?

He wanted to experience more pain
It was a sign of humiliation. Humbling himself.
It was normal for Kings to go barefoot.
His shoes were uncomfortable

It was a sign that David was expressing his humiliation and sorrow for the luxuries he experienced as king that, perhaps, were excessive. He was symbolically apologizing for the sins and, in the process, revering God and His holiness. King David assumed that he had brought this evil upon himself. I can't imagine a more touching sight. I am thankful that God allowed us to see the levels to which David was willing to go, and emotionally forced to go, due to his son's betrayal.

Now transport yourself to David's cave. A while later, David's men suggested that he stay separate from them for his safety. That's when he found a cave and wrote Psalm 3. Read Psalm 3:1-2. Can you hear the sorrow in his voice? In these two verses, who did he worry was against him?

_____

_____

_____

I have again listed the six core hurts. Look at them with David's moment in mind, and dissect for him what you think his core hurt might have been.

1. Fear
2. Anxiety/Worry
3. Disappointment
4. Loss
5. Pain (physical, emotional or spiritual)
6. Temptation

Although our answers could vary, what do you think David's core hurt is? Why?

_____

_____

_____

_____

We've spent time looking at David's moment, as well as Alan's. David learned that he was still a warrior, and that, through God, all things are possible. Likewise, many miraculous events took place to keep Alan's family business afloat for five more months. In that time, a buyer for the company was found, his dad was taken care of, the employees' jobs were saved, and Alan found his dream job. Now, it is time to look at your own situation.

Thoughts in the Foxhole:

Today, in the Foxhole, I want you to feel safe in God's love. Overhead, the enemy might be slinging arrows, but while you are alone in your Foxhole, he won't hurt you. I want you to think about your David Moment and peel away the layers. When I peel away the layers of my hurt, I envision a stinky onion. As I hold the onion (my David Moment) in my hand, all I see is a yucky, stinky mess. But, as I look at my onion, I think to myself, "My David Moment is about my son's health." Well, no, it's not. Peel a layer away. "Okay, it's about my wanting him to be happy and not hurt." I was getting closer, but not yet. Peel another layer of onion away. "It's about me wanting Collin to have a great future." I was closer still, but peel another layer away. I wasn't there yet. "It's about my worry regarding his life and future." Yes, but peel one more layer; I could go deeper. "I needed to have faith that God is involved in my son's life and is planning his future." Bingo! Not only was God planning a good future for Collin, the things that Collin is going through will be used by Him to create a powerful future. I had to come to the reality that faith was not a luxury. Faith is required, in order for me to let go of my son's hand, and allow God to put blessings in my open hand. Collin's future was not my responsibility; it was our loving Heavenly Father's.

It is now your turn to peel the onion layers away until you get to the heart of the issue. At the heart of my David Moment was worry and anxiety. What will yours be? Find out; start peeling!

_____

_____

_____

Lesson Three
Who Are We Fighting?

You may think your enemy is the person who hurt you, the pornography your husband is addicted to, or the illness that hurts someone you love. It's not. Your enemy introduced himself in the Garden of Eden as he explained why Eve should defy God. Our enemy has been lying, tricking, deceiving, and trying to destroy us, since the Earth began. One of the more convincing ways Satan does this is by getting people to believe he doesn't exist. Worse yet, he is great at convincing people that God Himself does not exist. But what Satan means for evil, our Heavenly Father can use for good.

Many years ago, when I was in college, and before I was a Christian, Satan initiated his fatal flaw in my life: He showed himself to me. I was a girl who loved getting scared and was fascinated with scary movies. An evening with a Ouija Board changed all of that for me. After that evening, I had no doubt that Satan existed, but the next day God helped me see that if Satan was real, maybe God was, too. I told my best friend at the time about my experience and he started praying vigorously for me. Soon after, I started going to church with him and I came to the realization that not only was Satan real, so was God and better yet, God won!!! And, oh yeah, I married that best friend in 1990.

In 1995, Alan, that best friend and now my husband, and I were running a city-wide marriage conference, and were having a meeting with our leadership team. My husband and I were talking and catching up with two men who had helped with the conference the year before. The first man was telling us about many tough things he had been dealing with over the past three months. The second man was a member of the Bikers for Christ group. He was at least 6'5", 300 pounds, wore leather from head to toe, and had a long beard. I have to say that, if you didn't know him, he would be more than a little intimidating, but in actuality, he is a gentle giant. Alan and I stood there with compassion and empathy, feeling bad that our friend was going through such tough times, but the smile on our biker friend's face grew with every mentioned problem, until he vigorously threw his hand on our friend's back and said, "Well, praise Jesus! You must really be doin' some great things for God, 'cause Satan sure is angry at you!" We all laughed so hard that people around us looked to see what was happening. To this day, when things go wrong in my life, I think back at that wonderful scene, and hope that I, too, am "doin' some great things for God."

Satan is real. He wants to interfere in our lives, in our relationships with the Creator, and with the great things God is accomplishing through us. Let's look at how he may have played a part with King David.

The King David Connection:

Satan is the author and creator of the six core hurts. He chose to separate himself from God, and desires to interfere with His perfect plan. We need to be willing to see Satan's interference in our lives, but we also need to be careful not to give him too much credit. I have seen too many people in my time who don't believe Satan even exists, but I have also seen Christians who see Satan in everything that goes wrong in their life.

Before we examine Satan's influence with King David specifically, we need to realize a few things regarding his character and influence. The first thing we have to keep in mind is that Satan is not omnipresent. Read Matthew 4:2-4.

Who is "the tempter"?

_____

_____

Which part of this passage suggests that Satan is not omnipresent? Why?

_____

_____

_____

_____

A being who is omnipresent would not have to "come to him." This is in sharp contrast to God's presence in the world—as seen in Psalm 139, God is everywhere.

Read Psalm 139:7-12. How is this different from the passage above where Satan "came to him?"

_____

_____

_____

Satan is not the counter equal to God. Many tend to treat Satan as the evil opposite to God. This could not be further from the truth. Satan is lower than God in every way, and has already lost the ultimate war of good and evil. It is interesting, though, that there are battles waging, and some yet to be fought, where Satan does fight. Read Jude 9 and Revelation 12:7-13.

In these two battles (one from the past and one in the future), who battles with Satan?

_____

So from these two points on the character of Satan, we have learned a great deal about his lack of divine power. Unfortunately, he still has great influence, which leads us to explore the power Satan does hold. Luke McKinnon of X Factor Christian church, explains that Satan has four forms of influence in the world: no influence, demonic influence, oppression, and possession. We will be focusing on demonic influence and oppression, because we know that Satan had influence in David's situation, but could not go so far as physically possessing him because David was protected by God, just as you and I are as Christians.

Demonic influence is an indirect attack. These are things that Satan and his demons do not have to be a part of directly. Sin was introduced into the world. The serpent showed Eve the fruit on the tree of the knowledge of good and evil, yet she still had to choose whether or not to take from it. That sin has been, and continues to be, a snowball that has the ability to grow in size, sphere, and influence in the world, and in our lives. Satan and his demons capitalize on that influence. They do not have to lift a finger to exercise it. One current example is the ease of which it is possible to get a divorce. There is even a store called _The Divorce Store_ that advertises the speed and ease of the end of a relationship. Let's look at King David's experience to see another example. Read 2 Samuel 15:1-4, 10:

What did Absalom conspire to do in these verses?

_____

_____

Have you considered what may have led Absalom to such a sinful obstruction of God's will? Read 2 Samuel 13:6-14. What happened here, and who was involved?

_____

_____

Read 2 Samuel 13:20-29. How much later did Absalom take revenge for his brother's attack of his sister?

_____

What did the passing of two years suggest about King David's punishment of his son's rape of his sister?

_____

Absalom was furious with his brother Amnon, but was it his place to avenge his sister? This revenge wasn't justice, it was usurping David's role as king, and ultimately refusing to wait for God's will to come about regarding the rape. The anger Absalom had regarding the rape and King David's refusal to punish Amnon left Absalom vengeful Absalom's anger provided the fuel that brought about the feeling that he would be a better king than his father. This, mixed with his desire to be king, was sin enough to provide for demonic influence. Satan and his demons did nothing directly. The many sins involved in the situation caused chaos and death for many.

Think back and list the sins, and consequently, the demonic influences involved in Tamar's rape and Absalom's conspiracy

_____

The second form of influence we will discuss is demonic oppression, which is direct external attack. Remember that, because of the Holy Spirit, Satan cannot internally attack Christians, (also referred to as demonic possession). However, Satan and his demons can externally attack Christians. One way they do this is through _____ (Matthew 4:1). David was attacked through a form of temptation, which can be found in Zechariah 3:1.

Satan stood on the right side of the accused, the High Priest Joshua, to do what?

_____

This could mean, that the purpose was to accuse Joshua as a prosecutor in a court of law, but it could also mean that he stood next to Joshua and whispered accusatory comments in his ear until Joshua believed him.

Read Psalm 3:1-2.

David was completely distraught. He kept thinking about how everyone hated him, how even God was against him. Was this true? If you need a refresher of the scene, read 2 Samuel 15:14-17.

_____

Did God ultimately deliver him? How did God change what David thought was happening? Take a sneak peek at the end of the story. Read 2 Samuel 18:28

_____

It is Satan's goal to destroy God's influence in our life, as well as God's influence in others' lives through us (our witness). Did Satan destroy God's plan for David? No, but he and his demons both indirectly and directly caused a lot of chaos, anger, revenge, and death. Thankfully, God prevailed, but a lot of hurt was involved in the midst of the battle. Are those same battles lurking in your life? Be aware, and be prepared!

Just like Eve, Satan might hand us the fruit and whisper in our ear how it is okay for us to eat it, but it is our choice to take it and eat. We have to beware of Satan and his schemes. Are you influencing people to Christ? If so, Satan isn't happy. Just like the biker at the beginning of our study today, keep marching, soldier, because if Satan is mad at you, you must be doing something right for the Kingdom of God! Let's go to the foxhole, consult with the General and come up with a tactical plan to keep us away from Satan's influence.

Thoughts in the Foxhole:

My goodness, the foxhole might be a busy one today! Remember, your foxhole is a place to safely think about, and meditate over what you learned today. One of the more difficult things to do in the midst of a crisis is to *stop*. I know that when I'm in a battle, my fighting instincts take over, and I try very quickly to fix everything. In 2 Corinthians 10:5, Paul tells us that we have the power to hold every thought captive to obey Christ, so we need to train our thoughts, inclinations, and desires; to stop and jump in our foxhole when a battle is underfoot. I'm not saying you should avoid the fight, far from it. Take the time to figure out what is really happening before you act, and, thus, be much more prepared.

Today in the foxhole, I want you to think about who or what you have been fighting. Have you been fighting your husband? Have you been fighting a disease? Once you realize what or whom you are fighting, you will be more equipped to strip it down. Most likely, it is Satan, the spiritual forces of darkness, as seen in Ephesians 6:12, you are truly fighting, either indirectly through demonic influence, or directly through oppression. When I have done this, it has led to some of my most joyous moments. Being used as a tool of the Living God, and watching Satan get mad and run away is an amazing privilege.

I thought I was fighting

_____

_____

I now realize that my true enemy is Satan, and that he has been attacking me through (demonic influence or oppression). Explain:

_____

_____

_____

_____

_____

_____

You have finished the first week! Congratulations. It has been packed with some difficult information to relive, process, and pray through. I'm so glad you did, because now you know what you are fighting, and the battle is very possible to fight. I hope you are also starting to see the extent to which God is by your side. He's in battle, in the foxhole, and even there when you are not sure what you need.

Week One
Battle Plan

Consulting with the General:

The General in your fight is our Savior and Lord, Jesus Christ. This is your opportunity to consult with Him. In the space below, let Him help you decide upon the David Moment you will use throughout this study. Ask Him for His help in seeing it clearly, yet through His grace, allowing the possible pain to be at arms-length. Our General has already won the war, and is sitting by your side. Grab the hand that is reaching for yours, and talk to Him.

Write your David Moment (or season) below:

_____

_____

_____

_____

_____

_____

_____

_____

_____

_____

_____

Your Tactical Plan:

A tactical plan is used in the military, when you are planning for a specific battle. Your battle (David Moment) is described above. You have also consulted with the General, and you have His perspective on what moment you will use to overcome defeat in the battle. Now you get a chance to act. Take the space below to write down what you will do right now with the information you were given during your time with Him. Test the words you heard against Scripture. Are they accurate and biblical? If you are unclear, always ask mature Christian friends to help you determine your next move, biblically. After alone time with God and biblical counsel, press forward. Your next move might be as simple as starting to rely on the peace of God for the first time in your life. But before anything else, we must allow God to establish our steps (Proverbs 16:9). Don't worry about what you have to do about this battle next week, tomorrow, or even two hours from now. Let God help you live right here, and right now. As it says in 1 Corinthians 16:13: "Be on the alert, stand firm in the faith, act like men, be strong." (ESV)

Right now, I plan to

_____

_____

_____

_____

_____

_____

_____

_____

_____

_____

WEEK ONE REVIEW

It is my goal during this study to help you dissect your David Moment, create a battle plan, and become a Warrior. There is a war going on. This war isn't against flesh and blood, but against the forces of evil in this world (Ephesians 6:12). Through deception, temptation, and accusation, Satan wants to pull you away from God and into the pit of despair, which will make your witness powerless; but we serve a God who has already won this war. As Christians, we can mope in our bedrooms, feeling alone and powerless, or we can stand with Christ and fight! Through the power given to me by my Lord and Savior, I choose to fight! Join me!

Discussion Questions:

1. Because of your David Moment, can you have true empathy for David?

2. How can the discovery of your David Moment help others?

3. Have you felt God's love in the midst of this week's lessons? Describe it.

4. Is there a core hurt that you experience more often in your life? What does God want you to do to eliminate this burden from your life?

5. How are demonic influence and oppression involved in your core hurt?

WEEK TWO

Gaining a Warrior Mentality

In the dead of night, she smuggled the child from the Warsaw Ghetto into her house. Tomorrow, she would move the sweet curly-headed three-year-old girl to Rodzina Marii Orphanage in Warsaw, where Irene entrusted frightened Jewish children to caring nuns.

"Where are we going, Miss Irene?"

Irene answered the child, "Sweet girl, you get to sleep here tonight. Tomorrow, you will go to a new, beautiful home." Just then, she heard a pounding on the door. Irene took a deep breath. "Sweetheart, I need you to hide under this floorboard and not say a word. I'll be right back."

She gently kissed the child and replaced the floorboard over the girl, who was only too used to this kind of scary sound as the pounding grew louder and louder. Knowing the authorities had been watching her, Irene walked slowly and purposefully as she said a prayer on the way to door. "Lord, please protect this child, and your will as I open the door. Let them see what you want them to see and no more."

As she reached for the doorknob she already knew what she would see. On the other side stood monsters beyond description. Before she even finished turning the knob, the door flung open and the monsters barged through the door. These monsters were dressed in the typical SS uniforms, but their true evil shown in their eyes and through their hearts.

"Where are the children? We've heard you have children!"

"Sir, I'm a single, thirty-year-old woman. I have no children, but look, if you must." After leaving their odor of cruelty around her house, they determined there were no children and left. This happened time after time for years.[1]

Irene Sendler was a Warrior. So many of us carve out a portion of our week to help others. I look up to women who put their own comfort and enjoyment aside for the sake of others, but what Irene did was far different. Irene put her very life on the line to follow God's will and save Jewish children in the Warsaw Ghetto, from 1940-1944. She refused to listen to her friends who referred to Jews as animals. She also refused to listen to the nuns, who were afraid for her safety, and, with compassion, asked her to stop. Irene put her fear aside, and dressed herself with the bravery of the Savior in order to do His will. She saved thousands of children, and died in 2008 at the age of ninety-eight. She once said, "We are not heroes. I continue to have qualms of conscience that I did so little."[2]

My own prayer is that I can gain that warrior mentality to do God's will, despite the cost. I look forward to hearing these words from my Savior, "Well done, good and faithful servant." Let's figure out how to gain that mentality together, as we go through this week's lesson. Here is what we will study

Lesson One: Stop Worrying and Start Trusting
Lesson Two: Fear Not
Lesson Two: Have Courage

LESSON ONE
STOP WORRYING AND START TRUSTING

"My child has a learning difference which makes it difficult to learn, so there is only so much he will be able to accomplish."

"I'm not a persuasive speaker. I'll embarrass myself and God. I'll let someone better than me tell them about God."

"Oh, I can't run that race. I've never run that far. I'll be a cheerleader on the sidelines."

"The cancer is too great. The doctors have given me too little chances of survival. I'll get my things in order."

"I have Bi-Polar Disorder. I keep trying to fight it, but it keeps winning. The fog always returns. God must not want me to be healed."

This is a difficult lesson for me to write. I am learning right beside you. I tend to worry about what people think of me, while trusting God and His will second. I admire people like Irene Sendler, John the Baptist, and Apostle Paul, who cared for the preciousness of others to such a degree that they didn't let worry stand in their way of listening to God's will. They listened to one voice: God's.

My list of worries is so long, that I could fill this book. It has been a long fight learning how to stop the inner dialogue of worry, and start trusting the One true voice. In order to be a good warrior, I've learned that I need to let God establish my steps (Proverbs 16:9). If I try to plan my own course, I grip at the problem so hard, that I can't grasp onto the blessings the Lord wishes to lavish upon me.

To be able to hand Jesus our worry, it is important to understand the difference between worry and anxiety. Amy Simpson, author of *Anxious: Choosing Faith in a World of Worry* defines worry as a prolonged state of anxiety. She says that both fear and anxiety can look the same, physiologically.

"Both can encourage us to get out of the middle of the street. Both can help us in the short term, but both can hurt us in the long term. Worry enters the picture when we choose to stay in a place of unease. Unlike normal anxiety, worry is not an involuntary physical response, but a pattern we choose to indulge. Whether or not we are conscious of it, worry is an action and a choice we make. We choose to stay in that place of anxiety that was designed to protect us from immediate danger." [3]

She goes on to explain that some people have an anxiety disorder. For these people, staying in a state of anxiety is not a choice. It is a disorder that rises when the body's healthy, helpful, biological process works overtime. It is essentially too much of a good thing. People who suffer from this disorder often deal with being misunderstood and deal with shame as a result. We should not allow with shame to occur. Anxiety disorder will is present in 29% of us at some point. Christians should wrap our love around our sisters with this disorder. [3]

We will see in this lesson that, for a moment, King David cries out regarding his dire situation. He is worried about what people are saying about him, he is worried that God's presence has left his side, and he's worried about whether or not he'll survive. In the process, his worry became a lie, he blinded himself to God's power, and his ability to reflect the power of God was weakened. After a time, he stopped worrying, and started listening to God. Let's delve into this study and see what happened to David. We will see how his worry almost took away his warrior mentality, but how trusting in the Lord helped him tap into the power of God!

The King David Connection

<u>Worries can make a lie become reality.</u>

Once you start worrying about a problem, your heart starts believing the lie (another little gift from Satan). Read John 8:44.

Fill in the blanks. (I use NIV)

> You belong to your father, the devil, and you want to carry out your father's desires. He was a murderer from the beginning, not holding to the _____, for there is no _____ in him. When he _____, he speaks his native language, for he is a _____ and the father of _____.

In life, we are influenced by our fathers. That is why fatherhood is such an important responsibility. If Satan is the father of lies, than we have a choice to be influenced by a lie, or by the truth.

I remember, as a child, eating alone in the school cafeteria. I had plenty of friends, but I distinctly remember looking around the room, finding no one to sit with, sitting alone, and then sulking. My inner voice of worry was speaking so loudly, that I couldn't hear Jesus telling me to make a new friend and sit with a new group. Instead, I sat alone the whole lunch time, and emotionally repelled anyone from coming close to me, hence bringing my worry to reality.

David also had a worry that became real. Read Psalm 3:1-2.
List two worries of David in these passages.

1. _____

2. _____

Now read 2 Samuel 15:18, and 2 Samuel 16:1-4.

1. The first worry I see is "How many are my foes." He feels as though everyone is against him. What verse from above proves this to be a lie?

   _____

2. David's second worry is, "Many are saying of me, 'God will not deliver him.'" What verse dispels this lie?

   _____

David was so consumed with worry and grief, he couldn't see that God was delivering Him. God was right beside him, taking care of him.

<u>Worries can blind you of God's power.</u>

So many times when we worry we don't see all of the things around us that God is doing to take care of the very worry we are obsessing over.

David was obsessing about everyone hating him and God abandoning him. This couldn't have been further from the truth. Let's first look at what God did to alleviate David's first worry:

Refer back to 2 Samuel 15:18.

How many troops left with David? _____

Read 2 Samuel 15:21.

Did David have devoted followers? Who? _____

Let's take David's second worry,: God had abandoned him. We've already established that God provided loyal troops to help David (2 Samuel 15:18), and supplies for David and his troops (2 Samuel 16:1), but He was also answering prayers.

Read 2 Samuel 15:31.

What was David's prayer?

_____

_____

Ahithophel had been David's counsel. When Absalom's conspiracy came to fruition, Ahithophel stayed with Absalom, and was no longer loyal to David.

Read 2 Samuel 16:23; 2 Samuel 17:14.

How was his prayer answered?

_____

_____

<u>When you worry, your witness (ability to reflect the power of God) is weakened.</u>

David kept voicing his worry. Everyone knew that David was worried that God's presence had abandoned him. The biggest problem with this is that David's people started believing this too.

Read 2 Samuel 15:30.

We hear David saying in 2 Samuel 15:26, that if God is not pleased with him, he is ready for what God will do. After a while, David's people started believing him. In 2 Samuel 15:30, what did the people join David in doing?

_____

Covering your head was a sign of mourning. According to the Benson Bible Commentary, going barefoot was a sign of captivity. "A more memorable event, surely, was never recorded in history, nor a more moving spectacle exhibited to mortal eyes! A king, venerable for his years and victories; sacred in the characters, both of his piety and prophesy; renowned for prowess, and revered for wisdom, reduced to the condition of a fugitive!"[4] His people may have been sympathizing with him. They may have been mourning alongside their king whom they loved, but at the heart of it, they believed what David believed. As was commonly done when someone was ashamed and confused (Jeremiah 14:3), the king's people imitated him. David's witness could have been one of strength and confidence in the Lord's plan, but in that instant, it was one of confusion and worry, and thus his people were equally filled with confusion.[4]

There is a simple and powerful remedy for worry.

Read Philippians 4:6-7.

What should you be worried about? _____

What three things should you do with your worries?

1. _____

2. _____

3. _____

What will happen when you do these things?

_____

_____

_____

Take a sneak peek at David. Read Psalm 3:3-6. Does he start doing these things? _____

How does David remedy his worry throughout these verses?

_____

_____

_____

Thoughts in a Foxhole:

Today is the day that we acknowledge our worries and hand them to our Father God. Fighting is most successful when we can concentrate on the battle, and rid ourselves of outside worries. Military professionals are taught early on how to focus on the task at hand, and take their thoughts captive. Today we start the same training. I want you to think about your David Moment and list the worries associated with it. Then, follow that with giving each worry to Jesus. In your mind's eye, and in your heart, watch Him crush each one.

_____

_____

_____

_____

_____

_____

When you put your worries aside, you are trusting our God, who is powerful enough to make everything out of absolutely nothing, yet He is compassionate enough to help a child make a new friend in the school cafeteria. Give Him your worries and let Him destroy them. He loves you dearly!

LESSON TWO
FEAR NOT

"The black wall was approaching us. I had seen dust bowls before but nothing like this. I scooped up my younger brother and made a run for it. As my little brother screamed, 'the world is ending,' I had to ignore my own fear and keep running. At first I could see 20-feet away, but quickly that measurement was getting shorter. As the black wall of dirt quickly approached, my limited sight vanished. It got so dark that when I put my finger to my nose I could see nothing. The black wall was completely blocking out the sun. For a moment I panicked. If I got lost, my brother and I probably wouldn't survive. While sand was pelting my arms, face and legs, I said a prayer for help. Each step made it more difficult to breathe and harder to walk. My feet felt like lead weights under the pressure of the dust in my lungs and the sinking of my feet in the dust. After forcing my legs to keep moving, I felt the fence to our property. Holding my brother in one hand and the fence in the other, we made it home. We survived." [5]

That is the story of "Black Sunday", April 28, 1935, in Oklahoma. Roy Gunn, Rogene Tribble and Ilene Andle, each dealt with fear. Fear for them, was something you could see, touch, feel, and taste. They each survived what would later be considered the worst of the dust bowl storms in history.

Fear is the response to an immediate (real, or perceived) threat. Fear, like anxiety, is a natural God-given capability that is designed to protect us from danger, however, we tend to allow fear to have a greater impact in our lives than God intended. Just like the black wall, fear is real! It is a living, breathing, adapting creature. Just like that dust storm, we often see fear approaching. We can run for it, but before we know it, the black wall of fear overtakes us and tries to block out the light of Jesus. We know, however, that the light of Jesus is always there. The choice is ours. Fear steals our joy and confidence in the One who can change everything: our Savior! Just like the big sister found the fence to guide her home, it is our choice to find our way by grabbing our Savior's hand, and to keep moving forward with confidence and trust in the one who will always lead us to safety.

You may know that "fear not" is in the Bible three hundred and sixty-five times. We can make a cute statement that God knew that we needed to hear it every day, but greater than that, God knows that life is scary, and He knows that fear will rear its ugly head, and try to incapacitate us. Every day, I need to be reminded that God is in control, and leading me home.

I have a dear friend who battles an illness. She hasn't battled it once or twice, she has battled it three times. Every time she finds that it is back, her fear is real. "What if it overtakes me this time?" I have had the honor of being with her once a week. We talk about God, we cry out to Jesus together, we share our thanks to Him and we walk for miles. She is a true Warrior, and I have learned what fighting looks like through her.

The most important thing I want you to learn in this lesson is that fear isn't something to push aside, because we think we aren't supposed to be afraid. When a warrior is contemplating her strategy in a battle, it is important to learn what she can about the one she is fighting, and to not underestimate her enemy. We know that Satan is our true enemy, but he uses fear to blind us.

So, ladies, let's take the blinders off and stare fear in the face. Let's take inventory of where fear is hiding in our inner beings, and then let's allow Jesus to clean house, grabbing our hand and leading us to safety!

The King David Connection:

I am struck every time I read Psalm 3. Let's review the situation; David is in a cave. He is afraid, alone, and hiding. He is humiliated. It is probably dark and uncomfortable in the cave. In his mind, he has lost everything: his son, his kingdom, his influence, his power, his friends, and his home. I can't imagine a darker time to live through. Just like the black wall of dust from the dust bowl of 1935, David is separated from everything he has known, and is completely lost.

I very much appreciate how honest and transparent David is with his fear. So often, we as Christians try to put on a nice face and pretend that everything is okay, even when our world seems as though it is falling apart. David's raw emotions are refreshing, and they help us learn how to conquer fear. Read Psalm 3:1-2 again. Think through it. What is David fearful of?

1. _____

2. _____

Let's compare this situation to another similarly dark circumstance in the New Testament. Compare and contrast read Psalm 3 and Acts 16:22-34.

The setting:

How are the two settings of these situations similar?

_____

_____

_____

_____

_____

_____

Both David and Paul, along with Silas, were in a sort of prison they couldn't leave. They were uncomfortable, in the dark, and it seemed as if their situation wouldn't change. David was distraught over what he had lost. You can make an argument that David was in a sort of emotional pain due to the friends and allies he no longer had, and most importantly, that God was not with him any longer. Paul and Silas were in an equally dark, uncomfortable place with the physical pain of being beaten.

Let's review the differences:

Do both men talk about their fear? _____

No, they don't. David did, but Paul did not. It could be that Paul and Silas didn't experience fear, but it could also be that Paul didn't record his fear, because he didn't consider it important to the story.

In the midst:

I love watching what God wanted to record about being in the midst of fear and trials.

Refer back to Psalm 3 and Acts 16:22-34. In one sentence—yes I know that this will be difficult–explain David and Paul's attitudes while they were in the midst of their fearful situations. Remember that the entire chapter of Psalm 3 was written while most of Israel was hunting David in order to kill him.

David's:

_____

_____

_____

_____

Paul's:

_____

_____

_____

_____

My takeaway from these two men of God was enlightening. In the midst of their plight, they both experienced discomfort, and probably a certain degree of fear, but it was their decision to have faith, which changed their attitudes and brought them peace. I have no doubt that our loving Father was sitting next to each of them, comforting them. Now, let's look at their responses, and their actions after they decided to have faith.

<u>The response:</u>

Re-read Psalm 3:3-4 and Acts 16:25. These verses pinpoint both David's and Paul's responses to their decisions to continue in faith.

David did two things. Each verse describes an action.

   1. (verse 3)

_____

   2. (verse 4)

_____

Acts 16:25 highlights two things that Paul and Silas did.

1. _____

2. _____

Sweet sister, many of us are ladies with a list. I love writing "to-do" lists. I have even been known to write things on my list that are already done, just to have the pleasure of crossing it off. Anyone else? I love that through these two situations of darkness and despair, our loving Savior tells us exactly what to do when we are fearful! I've made your "to-do" list for you.

1. Praise Him! This can be through praise songs, as it was for Paul and Silas, or as lists of thanksgiving that you post around the house and add to. King David spent this time reminding himself who God is, and what He had done for him.
2. Call out to Him! Use the beautiful voice God gave you! When you need Him, voice it… yes, out loud! When we converse with our Savior out loud, our voice has God-given power!
3. Pray! Share with Him your fears, your knowledge of Him, and your belief that He is in control.

The battle:

The actual battle has very little to do with David and Paul, but everything to do with God. Let's look at just a few things He accomplishes:

Through David (Psalm 3):

Verse 5: _____

Verse 6: _____

Verse 7: _____

Verse 8: _____

Through Paul (Acts 16):

Verse 26: _____

Verse 30: _____

Verse 33: _____

Verse 34: _____

God accomplished a great deal through these two battles! David sleeps (probably for the first time in weeks), fear goes away, he is motivated to fight the good fight, and he forgives those who are hunting him. For Paul, God shook the ground, causing the earthquake which broke the chains that bound them. In addition, the guard who once kept them in chains was saved, cleaned the wounds of Paul and Silas, and found true, God-given joy. Wow, that is what can be accomplished if you release your fear and allow God to fight your battles!!!

Thoughts in a Foxhole:

Cozy up in a comfortable place, and acknowledge your fears. There is healing that comes simply from shedding light on darkness. Our fear is darkness. Fear is something that seems uncontrollable in certain situations, but perfect love casts out fear. That perfect love was accomplished by Jesus on the cross, and the victory won when He rose from the dead. Acknowledge the fear you have experienced during your David Moment. You can also consider a fear that you battle daily. Write down your fears and then shed Jesus' light on them. He will start taking them away immediately.

*Remember, fear is our reaction to a real, or perceived, threat that is in front of us. For instance, standing in the middle of a bull ring with a bull ready to charge. Anxiety and worry is not seen in an immediate threat but rather in anticipation of a possible threat. In our example before, anxiety and worry might be felt when we are in the first row of the bull ring. We might have anxiety that the bull could jump over the railings.

_____

_____

_____

_____

_____

_____

I've heard it said that none of us are ever more than six feet away from a spider. I don't know about you, but that is terrifying to me! If I ran around my house and tried to find, and get rid of every spider, I wouldn't have time to do anything else. It would rob my life of joy. Fear is the same. Let's face it; life is scary. This side of Heaven is filled with situations, people, and worries that can create paralyzing fear. In fact, we are probably always within six feet of something that can produce fear. It's up to you. Are you going to allow every fear rule your life, or are you going to give God the chance to help you FEAR NOT, and go on with the joy He designed for you? Choose to fear not! Trust God and the plan He has for you!

Lesson Three
Have Courage

The soldiers from the 116th regiment, 29th division, company A, were courageous. They volunteered for the Army National Guard and comprised the first wave on Omaha Beach in World War Two. They stood in Higgins boats headed for their first battle in the war; as they stood ankle deep in a combination of sea water and vomit, they anxiously awaited the boats to get out of the torturous waves of the open sea. However, their reward when they were getting closer to shore was the barrage of gun fire. They knew that when the boat's ramp opened, letting them out into the water, the battle which they had long been training for would begin. Sure enough, seconds after the ramp opened, one hundred and two of the two hundred men of company A were dead. Out of those still fighting, two or three dozen were fighting in spite of severe injuries. Still, they fought. They didn't hide behind fallen soldiers and wait out the battle. They didn't spend time looking for places to hide. They kept moving forward. They fought to rid the world of evil, they fought to protect their friends, and they fought to protect freedom.[5]

The words "bravery" and "courage" have been used interchangeably in the English language, but these two words are worlds apart in their truest definitions. Bravery is an attribute of a person's character. Some people are born with the ability to face danger with little to no fear. Courage, however, starts with fear. As John Wayne, one of the most well-known cowboys of all time, explained courage as not allowing fear to control you, but saddling up, anyway.

Courage is not natural. It is not something that someone is born with. Courage requires a person to acknowledge their fear, deal with that fear, and do what's right, anyway. As a Christian, God gives us the perfect solution for dealing with our fear. Give it to Him! In exchange, He gives us His special armor, which is impenetrable to hostile forces. Ephesians 6:10-18 goes through a step by step explanation of each piece of armor, and its use.

In truth, I am not brave, but I've learned to have courage. I don't have courage because of anything that is inside of me or by brushing off fear. I have courage in my life simply, and only, because my Savior has given it to me. To be honest, the longer I am on this Earth, the more I realize that anything worthwhile has required me to depend on Christ. Through God-given courage, anything is possible, because as Christian Rap artist KB put it, "Christian's don't fight <u>for</u> victory, we fight <u>from</u> victory". (Emphasis added).[6] The battle is won. Trust Him!

My goal for today's lesson is to help you trust God in the face of danger, and to help you accept the God-given courage available to you. Stop trying to white-knuckle your fear, and trust God to help you face danger with the strength and courage in which He has already dressed you.

The King David Connection:

This is our last look at David while he is distraught in the cave. Things are about to change. Imagine you are in that cave with him, and as we finish up this week, we will have the warrior mentality to start fighting the spiritual battles that exist in our paths. How did King David dress himself in the God-given courage he was meant to have? Let's find out.

Old Testament courage:

Read Joshua 1:9 and fill in the blanks.

"Have I not commanded you? Be _____ and _____! Do not tremble or be dismayed, for the _____ _____ _____ is with you wherever you go." (ESV)

The word "strong" in the Old Testament Hebrew is *Chazaq,* which means to fasten upon, seize or cleave. The word "courageous" in Greek is *amats,* which means to be mentally and physically strong, bold, and solid. Contrast this with courage in the New Testament.

New Testament courage:

Something interesting to notice is that, in the New Testament, the word for "courage" in Greek changes to *Tharseo* which means to be encouraged, or of good cheer

Read John 16:33 and fill in the blanks.

(Jesus speaking) These things I have spoken to you, so that in Me you may have peace. In the world you have tribulation, but take _____; I have overcome the world. (NIV)

The New Testament doesn't mention a word that is almost always mentioned along with courage in the Old Testament. What words are missing? _____

This is very interesting! The missing words from the Old Testament are "be strong". Why are they missing? In the Old Testament, courage was something you had to cleave to, catch, or seize. It was something you had to grasp through strength. In the New Testament our courage isn't something we have to put on in our strength, we are able to grasp it through the power of the Holy Spirit. In both verses, Old and New Testament, courage comes from the presence of God. Once Christ died for us and rose from the dead, the Holy Spirit, and everything we need for courage already exists within us; we only need to acknowledge it, grasp it, and take a step of faith.

What is a step of faith? Jesus asks many of those He performed miracles on to take a step of faith. Read John 5:7-9.

Jesus asked a man who had been paralyzed for thirty eight years to do what?

_____

Read John 9:6-7.

Jesus asked the man who was blind from birth to do what?

_____

My point is this; both men were healed. The paralytic and the blind man were healed, but Jesus asked those men to exercise their faith by doing what could only be done if they were healed. Jesus asked a man who could not walk to stand, pick up his mat, and walk away. He also asked a man who was blind to walk over to the water and wash his eyes. In order to do these things, these two men had to have the faith that they were healed. In the same way, I believe that is what God is asking of us when we need to have courage.

1. We need to acknowledge that God is with us through the Holy Spirit.
2. We need to acknowledge that Jesus gives us what we need to be courageous.
3. Take a step of faith. Even when we are still afraid, we need to take a step toward the battle, knowing that the Holy Spirit is with us, supplying our courage.

King David put on courage. Refer back to the Old Testament definitions of "strong" and "courage". What David needed to do to get courage is different than what you and I need to do. What two things did David need to do? Re-read Psalm 3:3-4.

1. King David shifted his attention from his plight to His powerful God: "But you, ___ _____, are a _____ about me, My glory, and the _____ who _____ my _____".

2. King David cries out to God: "I was crying to the _____ with my _____, and he answered me from His _____ _____".

Personal opinion: How did David cleave to God?

_____

_____

_____

Personal opinion: How was David bold, strong, and solid?

_____

_____

_____

Isn't it amazing that we, as Christians, already have the courage inside of us to do anything that God has planned for our lives?! Jeremiah 29:11 reminds us, "For I know the plans I have for you, declares the Lord, plans to prosper you and not to harm you, plans to give you hope and a future."(NIV) Jesus knows our past, present, and future. His plan is perfect, which means He will be there beside you, supplying what you need, at the very time you need it. Be prepared to take that step of faith, because God is already there with His hand out, ready to steady your step and give you the courage to take the next one.

Thoughts in a Foxhole:

With your David Moment in mind, consider where you need courage. In essence, courage is an extreme case of trust and faith. Ask God where He wants you to trust Him.

Where does your fear end and courage begin?

_____

_____

_____

_____

_____

Week Two
Battle Plan

Consult with the General

The General has the power to take away all fear; let Him. We learned through the stories of both King David and Paul how to do exactly that. Walk away from this time today with your past fears eliminated. Let's look again at how these two men rid themselves of fear.

1. Praise God for the things He has done for you, and meant to you in the past. This should include where He worked powerfully, even during your David Moment. You can record any praise, but be specific. God adores your praise, and the exercise will help remind you to trust Him.

   _____

   _____

   _____

   _____

   _____

2. Call out to Him! Vocally shout to the Lord! If you have the strength, shout out what help you need, in order to stop the fear associated with your David Moment. If you only have the strength to shout out "Jesus," do it! There is power in the name!

   _____

   _____

_____

_____

_____

3. Pray. Hand Jesus your fears. When you hand them over to Him, they no longer belong to you. Your fears are in the hands of the One who is pure light. In His hands, fears disintegrate like snowflakes in the sun.

_____

_____

_____

_____

_____

Your Tactical Plan

Now, it is time to acknowledge that we have done away with worry and fear, and that we are ready to trust in Jesus and have courage. In the space below, write down your plan for the courageous step of faith that God is asking you to take regarding your David Moment. Also, consider the future courage you'll need. Make a personal plan for when you need to tap into the courage the Holy Spirit has already given you.

_____

_____

_____

_____

_____

WEEK TWO REVIEW

I am so in love with my God, who walks in the fire with me, who breaks my chains, and who holds my hand through life's most challenging times. My precious Savior died for my sins, but also hanging on that cross was my fear, my worry, and my doubt. The moment Jesus rose from the dead, He made it possible for my future to be with Him by my side forever. With Christ, all things are possible. I can gain a warrior mentality by trusting my Savior, letting go of my fear, and gaining courage. We are ready for the future and what it brings, because God is there already, preparing it for us.

This week's Discussion Questions:

1. Discuss what worry looks like. How is it different from fear?

2. What effect has worry had on your life?

3. We talked in this lesson about fear and how to eliminate it. Did you try to praise God, call out to Him, and pray to Him? Did it break any chains that have kept you bound?

4. Are you brave? Have you experienced courage before? Please describe these experiences. Discuss the difference.

5. Was King David brave, courageous, or both?

Week Three

God: The Powerful Protector

It is dark. It is completely and utterly black on the field in front of me. Smoke hangs low over the field, stealing the breath from my lungs. It is deafeningly loud, although I can hear every gunshot and painful cry that calls out. I am in a hole I dug for the only protection I could provide myself, and I am overcome by anxiety. Occasionally, light floods the field from fire dropped from an airplane overhead. I'm not sure if I appreciate the ability to see or not. For those short opportunities, I only seem to see the fear and worry that hangs low and powerfully over the ground. The short spurts of light bring life to the gunfire, the yelling, and the pain that surround me. The anxiety starts to overtake me like ants crawling over my body. I want to scream, run and claw my way out of this battle. Just as hopelessness starts to grasp my soul, I feel a gentle and sweetly warm hand touch my shoulder. I turn around to see peace and joy gleaming in front of me. This man is the most beautiful sight I've ever seen. The confidence, joy, and hope that He exudes travel up my arm and into my heart. All of a sudden I know that He is with me, and with Him, the battle in front of me is already won. He stands in front of me, becoming my shield as He helps me out of the hole I dug, and we walk through the battle to the other side. With Him, I know that all things are possible.

Although the above scene is a fictitious story of someone in a war zone, I have felt similar anxiety in the midst of my David Moment. I know that I am not the only one who has lived through this reality. During my David Moment, there was so much pain and hurt racing through my heart, I couldn't see how to maneuver through my battle. It took Jesus grabbing my hand and showing me His plan to get me out. My goal for you this week, is to see how God is in the battle with you and walking you through it. He is your powerful protector!

In week three, we will see how God is living powerfully in our lives right now. Even in the midst of our David Moments, our Heavenly Dad is standing next to us, protecting us. As a baby

Christian I was taught this concept. But as I studied the different ways He stands next to us and fights for us, I see how wide His powerful protection spans.

In Day One, we will learn what a shield looked like in biblical times, and how that visual helps us see what He meant when He asked us to put on the shield of faith. Then, we will go on to understand the different aspects of a shield, and the ways a shield can help us in battle.

In Day Two, we will discover *The Great I Am* and how He helps us yesterday, today, and tomorrow. Finally, in Day Three, we will see how our prayers and thought lives can unknowingly limit the size, scope, and power of God. God's power and ability to protect us are far beyond our ability to imagine. In Day Three, we will learn how to dream.

Lesson One: The shield of Faith
Lesson Two: God, The Great I Am
Lesson Three: Praying Audaciously

Lesson One
The Shield

Ephesians 6:16 describes the shield as follows: "In addition to all this, take up the shield of faith, with which you can extinguish all the flaming arrows of the evil one."(NIV) In ancient times, the shield was one of the most important parts of a Roman Legionnaire's armor.

The Greek root of this word is *thureos* meaning, "large door-shaped shield."[1] This shield was called a Scutum. It was approximately three and a half feet tall and three feet wide. It curved around the soldier in almost a cylindrical manner. The shield was usually made of wood, and was light enough to carry one-handed. It was constructed with three sheets of wood glued together, and then covered with leather and oil for durability. There were metal designs on the shield that would identify one unit of soldiers from another, but also helped make it an offensive weapon as well as a defensive tool, when pushed against an enemy. It is important to note that, due to its size and shape, a soldier could literally hide his entire body behind the shield.[1]

The Bible talks a lot about shields. Ephesians 6:16 refers to a shield as the faith we should grasp onto. Deuteronomy 33:29 talks about the shield as the help that God will provide in the midst of struggle; Proverbs 30:5 speaks of a shield being a place of refuge; and, finally, 2 Samuel 22:36 tells us that, through the shield of His salvation, we can accomplish great things for His glory. The beautiful aspect of a Biblical shield is that our precious Savior meant for you to realize that He, Himself, as a shield, is all of the above, and so much more. He is the author of our faith, our protector during struggle, our refuge from the fiery darts of the enemy, and our source of confidence and courage, which allows us to do great things for His glory.

When David was scared in the cave, he forced himself to reevaluate his circumstances. He was scared for his life, and felt as though his best friend and Savior had turned His back on him. Yet, in Psalm 3:4 he reminded himself of who God is, and what He had done for him. God had been his faith, his protector, his refuge, and his courage. God had been his shield.

Let's discover how God is your shield. Today, just like David, you can grasp onto that shield, and change your life.

The King David Connection:

Psalm 3:3 is a powerful and meaningful verse. Write Psalm 3:3 below.

_____

_____

_____

_____

_____

Now read Psalm 3:1-3. Do you fully see the change in attitude, fortitude and confidence? What are the three things in Psalm 3:3, which King David says about God?

God is a _____

God is my _____

God is the One who _____

Yes, God is our shield, our glory, and the One who lifts our heads, but we are going to explore the idea of God being David's shield. We are going to study four benefits of God being our shield, and watch how King David benefited from the shield, in the same way that we can today. Let's look further into the different characteristics of the shield, as discussed earlier.

The Shield of Faith

Read Ephesians 6:16. In this verse, it says that we should take up the _____ _____ _____. It goes on to say that, with that shield, we will be able to extinguish the flaming arrows of the evil one.

What are the flaming arrows of the evil one? I think it is easy to see that Satan wants to put road blocks in the path that God has for us, and we often look at these as large, flaming arrows. These arrows can certainly be large problems which arise in our life, but in addition, they can be everyday temptations and trials that we face. List some daily arrows we need our shield to extinguish.

_____

_____

_____

_____

_____

_____

_____

Personally, I can think of many arrows I ask my Savior to extinguish on a daily basis: worry, self-doubt, and more. Look again at Psalm 3:1-2. What arrows did King David need God to extinguish?

_____

_____

_____

_____

_____

_____

The verse says that the shield of faith puts out the flaming arrows. How does the faith you have in our Savior put out the arrows?

_____

_____

_____

_____

_____

_____

The Shield of Protection

Deuteronomy 33:29 is a long verse. Before we start to take it apart, read it three times. Each time you read it, write one small aspect that stands out, catches your eye, or describes the character of the verse.

1st time _____

2nd time _____

3rd time _____

   I wish I could be with you as your discuss your impressions. The overwhelming aspect of this verse that stood out to me, was how God is my protection in times of trouble.

We've looked quite a bit at what King David was going through. Troubled times indeed! What are some ways that God has been "a shield of David's help?" There are many which we have read in 2 Samuel 15-18. Write one situation where God protected King David, which stood out to you.

_____

_____

_____

_____

_____

_____

The Shield of Refuge

Read Proverbs 30:5 and fill in the blanks. The version I will use is NIV.

Every word of God is _____; He is a _____ to those who take _____ in Him.

I love the visual of "refuge" that is vivid in my mind. The visual that is in my mind is me making myself as small as possible, hiding behind a large rock, hoping that the "bad guy" doesn't find me.

Now, at any given time, that "bad guy" can be anything. That bad guy has been worry, regret, fear, uncertainty, etc. Describe your visual of refuge below.

_____

_____

_____

_____

In order to truly understand the idea of refuge, it is important to define it.

_____

_____

_____

_____

A refuge is a place, situation or person who keeps us safe. That definition is spot on, not only for my visual, but with regard to what was happening with King David.

What do we know about King David's refuge?

Where did it take place? It is commonly concluded that King David found refuge in a cave. Read 2 Samuel 17:27-29. What does Scripture tell us?

_____

_____

Refuge can also take on a spiritual element. In looking at our definition again, as a Christian, when are we safe and sheltered from pursuit, danger, or trouble?

_____

The answer to the above question can be found in Romans 8:28. "And we know that in all things God works for the good of those who love him, who have been called according to his purpose. (NIV)

The Shield of Salvation

Read 2 Samuel 22:36. What has God given David?

_____

What does God's help make David? _____

We tend to think of salvation in the context of the salvation given to us through the death and resurrection of Christ. The salvation we speak of here was in the context of David being in the throes of battle. It means rescue, safety, and victory.

What did David need salvation from? There are many correct answers for this. You can think broad or small, physical or spiritual.

_____

_____

_____

_____

There are two things that are striking which led to King David's victory against the insurrection of Absalom. Read 2 Samuel 18:3-4. David was given advice, which he humbly followed. What was the advice? _____

What can we learn from this example when we are seeking victory in a difficult situation?

_____

_____

It is important to pray for God to lead you to godly people when looking for advice, but then, with humility, you must follow through.

The second aspect of our shield of salvation is watching for God's divine intervention in our battles. I can't tell you the number of times I look back at a battle in my life, and see God's divine intervention. It is now my goal to watch for, and find, the times when God is in the midst of intervening in a problem. Read 2 Samuel 18:8 carefully. Try to really see the picture that the verse is painting. What does the text suggest was happening to Absalom's men?

_____

_____

_____

Yes, it could be that "the forest devoured more people that day than the sword devoured," (CSB) means that people got lost and died, but couldn't it also mean that God used supernatural means to kill David's enemy? It is an interesting thought.

Our Father in Heaven is our shield. He gives us faith, He protects us, He is our refuge, and He is our salvation and victory in battle. 2 Samuel 22:36 talks about God helping David in battle, providing victory and greatness. It was through David's humility, and love of God, that his greatness was even a possibility. When our sole desire is to give Christ the glory in our battles and in our lives, our successes will be merely a reflection of the beauty of our Heavenly Father.

Thoughts in a Foxhole:

Consider how your David Moment fits into each aspect of the shield. How would each aspect be helped by the shield?

Faith_____

_____

_____

Protection_____

_____

_____

Refuge_____

_____

_____

Salvation_____

_____

_____

There have been times when I felt that I have crawled behind a big rock to hide from the pressures of life. It was through the priceless lessons that my Savior has taught me through my David Moment, that I finally learned how to exchange the big rock for the shield of God. My confidence in who I am as a child of The Most High has exploded, and what I can accomplish through Him is infinite. So, grasp your shield, and realize that whether you need it for defense or offense, God's got this!

LESSON TWO
GOD: THE GREAT I AM

You are sitting alone, and, like a tidal wave, memories of your David Moment crash against the peace and joy you've accumulated. Things have not gone well today. It is possible that it is a bump in the road, but it is also possible that tragedy has struck. However you would characterize your David Moment, what can you do when the moment, or the memory of the moment, floods your thoughts and throws you off balance? Do what David did. Remind yourself who God is.

There are a multitude of names for God in the Bible. In her monologue, "Who's Your Daddy?" Priscilla Shirer, a powerhouse Christian teacher, reminds us that when you feel like you can't handle the road in front of you, remind yourself who you belong to. She then goes through a litany of names and characteristics of our Heavenly Dad. I love how she words her speech because, in it, she reminds us that our Heavenly Father has always been a part of our existence, and will always be a part of who we are as children of the Living God.[3]

Today, we are going to work with one of His names: the Great I Am. I grew up in the New Age faith; in my formative years, that name held particular significance. It was believed that, since God referred to Himself with that name, then we held a similar quality of power within ourselves. In essence, we were in charge of every aspect of our lives. I became a born-again Christian at the age of 23. My biggest connection to my new faith was understanding that *we* did not have that power and strength, that God alone had the ability to change and influence the world around us, and that without Him, we are nothing. That name, "I Am" became the anchor to my new faith. I didn't have to carry the weight of my life solely any more. The Great I Am, who was far more powerful, loving, compassionate, and all-knowing, was the Savior of my life. I was a slave no more.

We need to look into the "I Am" name to understand God to the fullest. It is present tense; this means that God is in the present tense yesterday, today, and tomorrow. This is a difficult concept for us humans, who see only a small part of the larger picture, to understand. I explain it this way: God's creation is like a photo mosaic. A photo mosaic is a picture which consists, not of brush strokes, but of thousands of tiny photos. God alone sees the entire picture, our life is merely a small photo among billions. In our tiny photo lives, we have dreams, desires, problems, struggles, and yes, David Moments. God sees these moments in our lives and places them with the dreams, desires, problems, and struggles of others, to form a beautiful picture. If we trust (have faith in) the great I Am, who is living in the past, present, and future, we can trust that He is creating a path for our lives that works everything out for our good, and His glory.

The God who exists in your yesterday gives you the gift of hindsight. For just a moment, look back at your David Moment. Do you see, in what was surely a horrible time in your life, the Great I Am working in and through it? I certainly see Him in mine.

The God of today holds your hand. He celebrates with you when things go well, and He cries with you when things go wrong. Don't ever forget that we serve a God who loved us enough to come to Earth and experience this world as a human. Jesus was one hundred percent God and one hundred percent man. He knows disappointment, He knows sorrow, He knows joy, and He knows pain. As you grow spiritually, you start to be able to see Him moving in your life as it unfolds. Look for Him in your day; I guarantee He is there in every moment.

When we worry about a future event, we are seeing that event play out in our minds. When we do that, we are envisioning a future, in our minds, without God. Therefore, that future event in which we are worried, oftentimes looks far worse than it would actually play out to be. If that event really did occur, it would happen with Jesus' comfort and help, because God is already in our future, preparing our path.

Thank goodness the Great I Am is my Savior, King, and guide through this life. Let's see how David uses this knowledge to change his attitude from one of despair, to one of encouraged dependence on the One who always was, always is, and always will be.

The King David Connection:

Let's start by becoming firmly acquainted with Psalm 3:3-4. These two verses highlight the change from David being sad and despondent, to David realizing that, with God, He will be victorious. Write out Psalm 3:3-4 in the space below.

_____

_____

_____

_____

Now close your eyes and think about what you just wrote. Choose one thing that stood out to you from the two verses.

_____

_____

_____

How do you think the one thing that stood out to you helped King David? Did it help him see God working in the past, comforting him in the present, or keeping him from worry in the future?

_____

_____

_____

How can you apply that one thing that helped King David to your own life, and to your own David Moment?

_____

_____

_____

Now, this is going to be fun. Let's dissect King David's past, present, and future, and compare it to these two verses in Psalms. Let's see where the Great I Am was, is, and will be in King David's life, through one of the most familiar stories in the Bible: David and Goliath.

We have all heard of the story of David and Goliath. Let's dig a little deeper into the story.

Read: 1 Samuel 17:4-7. Does it sound as though Goliath was able to be defeated through traditional means of battle?

_____

Read 1 Samuel 17:12-14.

How many sons did Jesse have? _____

How many sons were soldiers? _____

Within the eight sons of Jesse, where did David fall (from oldest to youngest)? _____

Read 1 Samuel 17:17-19

Was David fighting in the army? _____

Read 1 Samuel 17:26

What question is David asking regarding Goliath?

_____

_____

_____

I love David's attitude here. With the faith of someone his age he says, "For who is this uncircumcised Philistine, that he should defy the armies of the living God?" (ESV) He seems to be saying, "Who is this fool that he would challenge God's army? Of course he will lose!"

Read 1 Samuel 17:28.

Was David's brother happy to see him? _____

Thinking back to 1 Samuel 17:17-19, was David there to see the battle, or was he doing as he was told? _____

Read 1 Samuel 17:31-37

In David's story, he recently killed what animals?

_____

Did he take credit for the killing of the animals? _____

Read 1 Samuel 17:45-46

David goes up to Goliath with only a slingshot, while Goliath is heavily armed. David tells the Philistine what is going to happen to him. Does he take any credit? _____

Read 1 Samuel 17:48-49

This is the part of the story we are all familiar with; David's victory over Goliath.

Past

As King David sits in the cave, full of worry and despair he reminds himself who God is. Read Psalms 3. What is the first thing David says? Fill in the blank.

But you, O Lord, are a _____ about me,

The text does not tell us if King David was remembering moments in his past when God moved powerfully, but could he have been? Had God been a shield about him in his past? _____

Let's move on. Continue filling in the blanks for Psalm 3:3.

My _____, and the One who lifts my head.

Use the information from above in 1 Samuel 17 to pinpoint the verse which highlights the moment from David's past where God brought him glory.

_____

_____

Present

David uses God's presence in his life from the past, to help give him strength in the present. Read Psalm 3:2-4 and ask God to show you the moment when David realizes that God is with him right now.

_____

_____

_____

I think there are multiple correct answers, but the moment that strikes me, is when he speaks in the present tense, and says, "(you, God, are the) One who lifts my head." (Author's paraphrase.)

Think: In your own life, what does it mean to have someone lift your head? Write about a time in your life when someone physically lifted your head. Write the feelings you experienced when they did.

_____

_____

_____

_____

Isn't it amazing that we can get the same love, comfort, empathy, and courage from the Creator of the Universe?

Future

In 1 Samuel 17, it appears as though David never pictured the attack of Goliath without God by his side, but what about the other Israelite warriors? Read 1 Samuel 17:24-25. Were they confident in their ability to kill Goliath? _____

Why weren't they?

_____

_____

_____

They saw a battle between Goliath, a giant of a man, and themselves. They didn't see a battle between Goliath and God.

When you think about your battle, do you think of it as a battle between yourself and the enemy, or God and the enemy?

_____

_____

Read Psalm 3:4

What does this verse remind us (as it did David) we need to do, in order to endure the battle of today, so that we can have victory in the battle of tomorrow?

_____

_____

My Bible version (ESV) says that David was crying to the Lord with his voice. That crying can mean tears, but more commonly means to call out, proclaim, or invite. I love the image that all we need to do with our future battles is to invite God to handle them. Why wouldn't you? He is already there, preparing your path!

Thoughts in a Foxhole:

I have quite a bit for you to think about in the Foxhole today. Considering your David Moment (DM), do you see how the Great I Am brought you peace and affected the outcome? Think through these past, present, and future questions.

Past: Looking back at your DM, how do you see God was working in and through the problem?

_____

_____

_____

_____

_____

_____

Present: What are some of the ways you are influenced today, because you can see the comfort God gave you in the past?

_____

_____

_____

_____

_____

_____

Do you see God working in your everyday life? List some examples.

_____

_____

_____

_____

_____

_____

Future: What is a worry or fear that you can release as you realize God is in the future, preparing a path for you?

_____

_____

_____

_____

_____

_____

Lesson Three
Praying Audaciously

I've prayed for my husband, the immense pressure he is under, and the hard work he goes through to provide for our family. I've prayed for my children's education, and for their social relationships (and let's face it, who doesn't pray for their child every time they get behind the wheel of a car. My children are fantastic drivers, yet that still terrifies me. I want Jesus right beside them.) I've prayed for my parent's health as they start to age and for my husband's parents, as they enter later years. I've prayed for the stresses and pressures my friends are going through, as well as my unbelieving friends' salvation. I pray for the accident I see as I drive down the street, and I pray for things I am dealing with in my own life. But one simple question from a guest preacher at a church we attended changed everything for me.

"What aren't you praying for?"

That's a simple enough question. When he first asked that, I thought, "Easy: Nothing!"

You see, I am a prayer. I even pray as I walk up to the phone, asking God to help me answer whatever is needed in the way He would like. Then the pastor continued.

"Is there anything in your life that you have held off praying for: big things, things that are so big they must be God's will?" Then he was quiet, and let an auditorium of hundreds of people mull this over. Like a bolt of lightning, it occurred to me.

I've prayed for my son's current medicine to work well. I've asked for the new doctor to understand him as a person. I've prayed that his seizure disorder won't interfere with school. I've prayed for his teachers to "get him." I've prayed for the insurance to pay for a brand name medication when the generic didn't work. But up until that moment, I had never prayed for my son's full and complete healing.

As I sat, dumbstruck with this realization, I look around the room and saw that many others had the same reaction. The pastor went on to ask us, "Why? Have we accepted second best? Are we worried His answer would be 'no?' Is it just too big for God?"

That was when I started learning how to pray audaciously. I now pray for all those things I prayed about before, but now I've added a few other prayers. I pray for my son's brain. I physically lay hands on him, and pray for his full healing. It is a mind shift to not only understand that God is all-powerful and capable of anything, but to also live my life in that reality.

At this point, I believe in the core of my being that God is going to heal my son; however, through his illness he is learning things that God will use powerfully when he is older. If He healed Collin right now, it is possible that my son wouldn't be prepared for the path that God has set in front of him. We have discussed this concept as a family, and he now wears his disorder with humble pride and graciousness, because God chose him, specifically, for something that he is being prepared for now.

We are going to look at audacious prayers in the Bible, and compare them to David, and how he used prayer in what seemed like an impossible situation.

Hold onto your hat for this one. It's going to be a fun ride!

The King David Connection:

The Bible is God's Word, and as such, it is full of awesome information; inspirational messages of hope, important advice, and stories that can teach us lessons. One of my favorite stories in the Bible is found in Joshua 10. I want you to read some of this yourself, but I am going to give you some background to get you started.

Joshua and the Israelites had taken over the land of Canaan (modern day Israel), one city at a time. They had already taken Jericho, and had successfully gone against Ai. At one time, the King of Jerusalem was unafraid of the unassuming force of Israelites led by Joshua, but now they had his attention. The King got four other neighboring kings together, and formed an alliance to go against this force. Little did they know, they weren't fighting a small group of fighters, they were fighting the One who created it all. The Israelites heard about this union of kings, and pulled a surprise attack with the help of the Gibeonites, with whom they had formed an alliance.

Read Joshua 10:7-14

In verse eight, what did God tell Joshua that gave him confidence?

_____

_____

_____

_____

_____

_____

Verse nine gives us a peek at the stress these fighting men were under. Read the verse again, and write down what was happening.

_____

_____

_____

_____

Yes, these men had travelled all night long, and then, without any rest, surprised the five kings in battle.

Fill in verse ten:

The Lord _____ them into _____ before _____.

The end of verse ten says that the Israelites defeated them. The enemy got scared and went on the run. The Israelites went on the chase.

Read verse eleven. What did God do next to help them?

_____

_____

At this point, I'd like to set the scene for you. Joshua and the Israelites had battled long and hard. They secured a victory that shouldn't have been possible, and they knew that they have to win completely. The sun is going down on a very long day, but if they don't finalize this battle with a complete decimation of the enemy, they know they will regroup and return. This is not an option. At this point, Joshua looks up at the sky, prays to God in front of his troops (with complete confidence) saying what? (Hint: look at verses twelve and thirteen.)

_____

_____

_____

_____

_____

_____

Joshua, with the confidence given to him by God, asked the sun not to set, and it didn't, for another full day. Now that, my friends, is an audacious prayer. Honestly, I hope that I would have confidence in battle if God told me He was beside me, but I'm not sure I would think to ask God to delay the setting of the sun. This is a constant reminder to me to not allow myself to limit God!

There are more audacious prayers in the Bible. It would be fun to do a self-study to find some of them. Let's look at King David's audacious moment.

We have learned a great deal about the scene in Psalm 3, and the level of King David's despair. In order to fully grasp the audaciousness of Psalm 3:3, we must see the contrast from verse two. In the space below, write your impression of the vast difference in David's attitude between Psalm 3:2, and Psalm 3:3.

_____

_____

_____

_____

_____

Have you ever been in the absolute pit of despair, and changed your outlook and attitude in an instant as David did? I would venture to say that if you have, it is rare. This is the kind of shift that is possible only through the grace of God.

Read 2 Samuel 19:8. Fill in the blanks.

So the king got up and took his _____ in the _____. When the men were told, "The king is sitting in the gateway," they all _____ _____ _____. Meanwhile, the Israelites had fled to their homes.

The gate, or gateway, was where a king would sit and administer justice. King David had locked himself away for quite a while. It might be difficult to understand for some, but no matter what his son had done, David still loved him. When Absalom died in battle, King David mourned. The verse you read above was the moment when the battle was over, King David and his men had won, and King David was declaring his role as King.

When it says that all the people came before him, it was their opportunity to congratulate the king, and declare their allegiance.

At the beginning of Psalm 3:1, we see that David was truly lost. The city, its people, the land, and those in authority, wanted King David dead. From that moment to the view in 2 Samuel 19:8, we see an audacious victory that could only be imagined and created by God.

Reflecting on Joshua's battle and King David's battle, what similarities do you see? I'm not needing you to go back and do heavy research on both stories, just sit with these stories, and allow yourself to see where God moved powerfully. If your mind floats to your own David Moment, let it.

_____

_____

_____

_____

As Christians, we pray; many of us pray a great deal throughout the day. God is always there, listening and communicating with us. Communication with our beloved Creator is always a two-way conversation, and he always answers our prayers. Sometimes, He answers with a quick and definite, "Yes!" Sometimes He answers with a, "Not yet." And sometimes He says, "No." Whatever the answer, it is important to not limit God to our preconceived idea of how a situation can, or should be handled, through our limited human concept of right and wrong. Petition God; this is never wrong. Pour out your heart; tell Him your fears and worries. Then let the Artist who created the flowers, mountains, and oceans, take your desires and put them in line with His perfect plan for you. His plan is more beautiful, perfect, and awesome than you could ever dream!

Thoughts in a Foxhole:

Today in the foxhole, think about those things about which you would like to petition God. Choose broad details, and then allow yourself to think outside the box. Is there something you haven't prayed for?

_____

_____

_____

_____

_____

_____

_____

_____

_____

_____

Week Three
Battle Plan

Consult with the General

Spend time alone with God, and ask Him to help you dream. God loves it when His creation realizes the extent of His power, and allows themselves to dream about what God can do in their lives. God can heal a broken marriage, he can heal sick children, and He can make the sun stay up for two straight days (ask Joshua). Write in the space below where you feel God is leading you to pray audaciously.

_____

_____

_____

_____

_____

_____

_____

_____

_____

_____

_____

_____

Your Tactical Plan

After consulting with the General, and prayerfully deciding on your focus, find a verse or several verses in the Bible, which will help you with your past, present, or future battle plan. Do you need God's help to see how He worked in your past? Do you need to spend more time seeing His presence in your daily life? Do you need His help preparing for a future battle?

_____

_____

_____

_____

_____

_____

_____

_____

_____

_____

_____

_____

Week Three Review

This week's Discussion Questions:

1. Is there an aspect of the shield that you need most?

2. Discuss the different aspects of the shield, and how they can aid in our daily lives.

3. Discuss how God can currently live in the past. How can this be helpful in our lives?

4. If God is preparing a place for you in the future, can he still manipulate your past to help with your future?

5. Can you think of other stories in the Bible that include audacious prayers, or people who lived audaciously?

WEEK FOUR

Spiritual Boot Camp

When you started this study, you may have thought you were going to join a nice Bible study, have coffee with friends, and enjoy Christian fellowship. What I hope you have learned, is that you have been involved in a battle of epic proportions for quite some time. During this study, you are learning what your personal battle looks like, who your enemy is, how to put fear aside, and how to trust our God, our shield. The second half of this study is going to teach you mental toughness in battle, how to fight, and how to celebrate the victory that has already been won.

This week, we are going to be in spiritual boot camp. When you enlist in the military, you first have to make the decision to join, but then there are a host of other things to be done, both physically and mentally. My friends, don't ever forget you are a warrior. Up until this moment, you may not have realized it. You may have gone to church on Sundays, and even studied your Bible with some degree of regularity; but ladies, our presence is requested on the battlefield. We can choose to get back on the bus and pretend that nothing is happening, or we can look this challenge in the eye and realize that our loving and powerful Savior is right beside us, preparing us, and guiding us through battle. So get off the bus, check into book camp, and join us.

The story below is a true account of what to expect in boot camp. It is written by Grayson Lee Trussell, Captain, United States Navy (retired). You may find striking similarities to how the Lord has been training you.

"The "Boot Camp" in military terms is designed to take the mostly young, inexperienced individual and teach him/her the rudimentary aspects of the military environment – the objective is to begin the creation of a combat capable "warrior." This mentally and physically stressful process involves testing the limits of the body and mind of the, often young, individual. It puts them in a situation that is usually totally foreign to their life's experience to date. Generally, this "learning experience" is provided to discover the weak and less capable and unwilling before they reach the battle field. Although it is impossible to fully predict the behavior of an individual in a frightening, often chaotic and possibly life threatening environment this early personal development conditions the successful individual to meet the basic challenges and responsibilities of an extreme situation – nothing will completely prepare one for the conditions of war. My own experience of Officer Candidate School (officer boot camp) and 30 years in Naval leadership positions and combat operations have proven this principle time and again - better prepared, to be better prepared, to be better prepared is the strongest characteristic of a proven warrior, which creates and supports faith in a higher source and confidence in the training received to meet and succeed at any endeavor."[1]

The point of military boot camp is to bring an individual to the end of themselves, then teach them that glory comes from obedience to the greater cause. Ladies, if this doesn't help us understand where we are and where we want to be, I don't know what will. Just like with military boot camp, we are transforming from naive, innocent 18-year-olds to powerful women, who will run toward the sounds of imminent danger, because we know we can trust the One who gives us strength. Throughout this study, we have been learning how to allow God to transform our David Moments from misery and fear to victory in Christ and glory for God. This week, we are in spiritual boot camp. As we learn to listen to Him, trust Him, and follow His words, we will not only win the battle, we will learn how God won the war.

Lesson One: Listening to God
Lesson Two: The Lord will Establish Your Steps
Lesson Three: Suddenly…

LESSON ONE
LISTENING TO GOD

I have a daughter in college six hundred miles away. Although her "home" is now in Oklahoma, we are closer than ever. How? We talk every day. My daughter is fiercely independent, resourceful, and capable. She has learned how to trust God in her daily life. In me, she has a trusted friend to cry with, celebrate with, and bounce ideas off of. The trust I have garnered from her is one of my greatest joys and honors.

With the first word that leaves her mouth, I can tell you if she has had a good day, a sad day, a maddening day, or a super spectacular day. Within the first moment of the phone call, I can tell you if we are crying, celebrating, or brainstorming ideas. Within the first sentence, I have deciphered whether she needs my help fixing a problem, or just needs me to listen and empathize. How do I know all of this? We have spent her entire life building this relationship.

Do you want to have that same type of relationship with Jesus? Great, me too; build it. I wish I could say I have spent the same number of hours talking to my Heavenly Dad as I have with my daughter, yet I can tell you this; the more often I spend time with Him, the more time I want to spend with Him, the more often I sit and listen to Him, and the more easily I hear Him.

I do communicate with my Heavenly Dad; it is a two-way conversation. I thank Him for what He is doing in my life, I pour out my heart to Him, I ask for Him to intervene in areas of my life, and I ask Him questions. Yes, He answers those questions.

The first time I was told I could ask God questions was in a sermon regarding Psalm 46:10, "Be still, and know that I am God." (ESV) To "be still" in this passage means to quit striving. It is to let go of earthly desires, struggles, and fears, and know that God's got this. If you pair this with another "still" from Mark 4:39, "Peace! Be still," (ESV) you have an interesting combination. Jackie Trottmann helps us visualize this verse. It takes place when Jesus is exhausted from the day, and falls asleep on a boat with His disciples. A sudden storm hits the waters and enormous waves appear. His disciples, in fear for their lives, wake Jesus to handle the problem. Jesus awakes, and yells at the storm (although it doesn't explicitly say in the Bible, I hear a little irritation in His voice), "Peace, be still!" This "still" refers to being quiet. So, putting both verses together, to be still means to sit, be quiet, quit striving, and know that God can handle any problem or question put in front of Him.[2]

It is one thing to know what it means to be still with God, but in our hectic modern lives it is quite another to actually put this into practice. A dear friend and sister in Christ helped me see this early in my Christian walk. We got together for lunch one day, and she asked how my week was going. I answered her with the litany of things that I had been working on, things I had gotten done, and things I couldn't seem to get off my "to-do" list. I was taken aback when she looked sad and told me that, as women, and for some reason, as Christian women, we put a great deal of emphasis and self-worth into being busy, yet this is directly contrary to what God wants for us and from us. For the twenty years following that conversation, I have worked on *not* being busy, which brings us to learning how to be still.

When I am wanting to hear God, I go to a quiet part of the house. During these times, I don't answer the phone, or questions from the kids (when my kids were young, I did it when they were at school or napping). Then, I quiet my mind. This takes practice. During any given day, we have an average of 50,000 thoughts which pass through our minds; getting them to stop takes patience and time. Once my mind and body are still, I start talking to God. When I was first learning what His voice sounded like, I would start my time asking Him to quiet other voices (i.e.: myself or Satan), and only allow me to hear from Him. After talking and pouring out my heart, I ask Him my question. Then, I wait. Sometimes, He answers me immediately, and other times it is after a few minutes, but He always answers me![3]

How do you know the answer is from God? There are three things you can do. First, test it against Scripture. In 2 Timothy 3:16-17, Paul says that the Bible is the Holy Word of God, and is inspired by Him; thus, God will never contradict Himself. Second, Proverbs 11:14 instructs us to seek godly counsel. Explain to godly people, whom you trust, what you've heard; seek their wisdom. Third, Colossians 3:15 shows us that, when we follow godly instruction, we will have peace in our hearts.

Our study today will have us compare two godly men, help us see how they listened to God, and the victory that God brought through their diligence to listen.

The King David Connection:

There are many godly people in the Bible who hear and follow the words of the Lord, but we are going to focus our study on two strikingly similar stories: King David and Elijah. At this point, you are familiar with the story of King David, so let's study this great prophet Elijah.

Read 1 Kings 19:1-18

Verse three says that Elijah was afraid for his life. Why?

_____

_____

_____

_____

_____

Record from verse nine where Elijah went, and what he did.

He went _____

He spent _____

Between verses nine and eighteen, the Lord speaks to Elijah four times. What does he say?

First time:

_____

_____

Second time:

_____

_____

Third time:

_____

_____

Fourth time:

_____

_____

Did Elijah answer him each time? _____

Did Elijah obey God when he was asked to do something? _____

One of the trickier things to do is to obey God when you still have doubt whether or not it is God, Satan, or you speaking. So, it is important to learn to discern God's voice, but it is also important to follow through with what is asked of you. Part of giving your life to Christ when you made a decision to follow Him, is to actually give your life to Christ! I have been there when God has asked me to do something I found uncomfortable, and then I talk myself into believing it was me, not God, speaking, and therefore I had no need to follow through. But oh, my dear friends, the blessings that exist when we DO follow through are life changing. Just ask Elijah.

Read verses 11-13. Four powerful things happened on the mountain. These verses take the time to emphasize each event. Write them down below:

1. _____

2. _____

3. _____

4. _____

God was not in the powerful wind, the earthquake, or the fire. God whispered to him. So often, we look for God in the dramatic moments of our lives and, all along, through everything, God can be found whispering in our ear. We serve a personal God who protects and sustains us through the big, awful moments of our lives, but He can always be found by one's side. In our society, we tend to listen to the people or events that are big, dramatic, loud, and carry the biggest stick, but society and the world can be changed in a whisper. Our job is to talk to God so often that we can hear our Lord whispering through the winds, earthquakes, and fires of this life.

Does this story of Elijah sound familiar? There are some striking similarities between this story of Elijah, and the story of King David that we have been studying. Brainstorm and list the similarities you notice between these stories below, and then we will look at the stories together.

_____

_____

_____

_____

_____

What was happening in both men's lives?

_____

_____

Where did both men go to hide from their fears?

_____

Did God show up supernaturally for both men? _____

How?

For Elijah:

_____

_____

For David:

_____

_____

There are many similarities in these stories. Both men were afraid for their lives, because there were powerful forces trying to kill them. Both men hid in a cave seeking refuge. God intervened powerfully for both men. For both Elijah and David, God provided physically for their needs. Also, God spoke to, and was heard by, both men. For Elijah, God was heard in a whisper during great tumult: wind, earthquakes and fire. For David, during the battle for Jerusalem, a great number of Absalom's men were swallowed up by the forest. God provided the victory for David and his men. Finally, for both men, God provided peace. This also highlights an important difference in the two stories.

Read Psalm 3:1-2. Does it sound like David is experiencing God's presence? _____

Read 1 Kings 19:4-5. Yes, Elijah was tired and weary, but was he experiencing the presence and consequently, the peace of God? _____

I believe that when David slept in Psalm 3:5, it was only after he had finally realized that not only was God by his side; He had never left him. From the start, Elijah was able to experience the peace of God, and enjoy His provision.

Here's the lesson that I am gleaning from these verses: God never left David's side. God provided loyal troops to be with him. God provided loyal friends to bring chaos to Absalom's reign. God provided food and drink, and God provided protection for David. However, David was not able to have the peace and joy of experiencing these provisions while they occurred, because he got lost in the fear, worry, and despair of his circumstances. Elijah, on the other hand, was able to experience God's provisions as they were happening. God provided food and a place of refuge for Elijah, and he was able to have peace enough to sleep in spite of his discouragement. You see, Elijah's discouragement was no less real and all-encompassing. Elijah was weary enough to pray that God save his life, and Elijah knew God was there. He knew that God wasn't in the powerful wind, the earthquake, or the fire. Elijah had the peace and joy of hearing God in the whisper.

Oh, friends, how I want to be Elijah; yet, through my David Moment, I can completely relate to King David. As I've said before, in the midst of my pain, I was unable to see where God had provided for me throughout the entire ordeal. Not only was God whispering to me, He was shouting, but I was so lost in my hurt that I couldn't hear Him. It wasn't until a month later when I was still, and with God, that I heard Him, and in His mercy and precious grace, my Heavenly Daddy didn't get mad at me; it was quite the opposite. He showed me where He had been through every moment, and then He held me while I lamented the loss of not experiencing His presence at the time. My friends, we serve a powerful, yet tender and loving God. Be still with Him, and experience the joy of hearing Him.

Thoughts in a Foxhole:

Reflect on the times in your life when God spoke to you, and you heard Him. Take the time to record one of those times.

_____

_____

_____

LESSON TWO
THE LORD WILL ESTABLISH YOUR STEPS

Joshua Hurley was finally able to attend his elementary school's required fifth grade camping trip. They would hike the wilderness, scale thirty foot walls, and balance along an exciting aerial ropes course. To say, "required," is over-reaching, because everyone looked forward to this annual overnight experience. He remembered when his sister went, and how excited she was to share all the stories she brought home. The whole family enjoyed her trip. Now it was his turn. The first day went well. Friendships were going well, the sleeping arrangements were fine, and the food was passible. He had even already collected a few stories to bring home. The second day brought a story that neither he, nor his family, would soon forget.

It was time for the orienteering class. This was annually a lesson that held a little more anxiety than the rest. All of the children were divided up into pairs, and given one compass to share. The leaders gave the kids one last lesson on how to read it, as well as the instructions of where they needed to go, and when they should be back. The kids were told to keep looking at their compass. If they were even one step off, they were to stop and reevaluate where they were, and how to get back on track. Even though Joshua listened intently, he wasn't worried. He had been camping with his family since he was born and was a Cub Scout; he was ready for this.

He and his friend started off on their adventure with a compass in hand and excitement in the air. The two ten-year-olds did just as they were told. They kept an eye on their compass and concentrated on the task at hand. An hour into the trip, Joshua did his routine check and found that they should be at their turn-around point, but they weren't.

"OK, no problem, time to reevaluate."

By the time Joshua and his friend should have been back, they had reevaluated twice. After the fourth reevaluation, they were three hours late and scared. The sun was hanging low in the sky and things were getting serious. Joshua thought he knew what he was doing. He thought he was the expert. How could things have gotten so off course? Joshua stopped and reevaluated his plan.

He had done everything he knew how to do. What should he do next? Then it occurred to him. Pray. He may be out of ideas, but the Idea Maker was just getting started.

Joshua turned to his friend and asked him if he went to a church that prays. When he said yes, both kids got on their knees in the middle of the forest and prayed to their Holy Father. With their prayer complete and hope reignited, they agreed they were supposed to go north.

Not five minutes down their new path, they saw a plume of smoke. They followed the smoke and found that it was coming from a chimney. Relief flooded them. They ran to the cabin, introduced themselves, and with exhaustion and elation were able to make the phone call needed to contact the camp leaders.[4]

Have you ever been lost? There are two ways you can be lost: You can be physically lost, just like Joshua, but you can also be spiritually lost. Although each of these have wildly different manifestations, they all have something in common. When we are lost, our Heavenly Father is the only one who can see the whole picture and get us home. Proverbs 16:9 says, "In their hearts humans plan their course, but the Lord establishes their steps."(NIV)

I have been physically lost before, and I have also been spiritually lost. If it weren't for my Heavenly Dad, I would still be checking my compass, reevaluating, and depending on my own frail human heart to get me home. Thank the Lord that I realized my expertise was spent, and I needed to depend on the Creator of All to establish my steps and get me home. Today, we will learn what "lost" looks like and what it means to depend on the Lord to establish our steps.

The King David Connection:

Being lost is terrifying. I, like most of you, have had that moment where I didn't know where I was--I was lost. The first emotion I felt was disbelief, then it was the realization that I was lost, but I still thought I had the knowledge to get myself out of the mess I had made. Finally, I started to feel warm, and a little panicky, realizing that I was truly lost. Unfortunately, we often have to go through all the other steps before we come to grips with the fact that we don't know where we are, and that we need help. There are three ways that we can be lost and the Bible talks about each; however, the common thread to each is that the only way home is God.

When we are fighting a battle, as we all are, it is important to quickly recognize our misdirection and trust God to direct our steps. Proverbs 16:9 reminds us, "In their hearts humans plan their course, but the LORD establishes their steps."(NIV) We are going to concentrate our study on the word "establishes." In the NIV translation, the word is "establishes", and in the NASB translation, the word is "directs." Write down the definitions of these words.

Establish:

_____

_____

_____

Direct:

_____

_____

_____

Quite often, I relate mental pictures to certain verses. These pictures are the visual I see when I read it. My initial picture of this verse was quite simple. I pictured my Heavenly Dad lovingly grasping my shoulders and turning me in the direction He wanted me to go, but after I looked at the definitions of these two words, I saw much more. God is the One who places our feet where they are in the first place. God makes our feet able to withstand the rugged terrain which we will face on our path. God controls what will happen to our steps and where they will fall. And yes, our Heavenly Dad, when needed, lovingly grasps our shoulders and points us in the direction we should go. Does that change your mental picture of the verse, as it has mine?

<u>Physically Lost</u>:

Read Luke 15:11-24

Who physically removed himself?

_____

_____

Yes, he was lost spiritually as well, but why did he not return home sooner?

_____

_____

Was he really lost, or was he choosing to stay away/hide from home?

_____

_____

What reaction did he anticipate from his father?

_____

_____

What reaction did he get?

_____

_____

Let's reflect upon what we know about King David.

What is similar between the Prodigal Son and King David?

_____

_____

_____

_____

_____

For both the Prodigal Son and King David, both men were dearly loved and cared for by their Father. Another interesting idea is that both men were more in self-imposed hiding, rather than lost.

Reflect on your David Moment. Remember, we are going to expose where and how we got lost, then let God establish our steps. When we are in battle, we don't have time to hide. Just like King David and the Prodigal Son, God has never left you alone. You may have thought that you were hiding, but God knew where you were, and He was establishing your steps, even when you were misdirected.

Spiritually Lost:

We are spiritually lost when we don't let God play a role in our life. Yes, that happens before we make a decision to follow Him and have a relationship with Jesus; however, it is overwhelming when we have a relationship with Christ, and a situation leads us to developing a self-imposed exile from His presence in our lives. The Prodigal Son chose to leave and was physically lost, but being spiritually lost can be paralyzing. When we are spiritually lost, we can feel alone like no other time in our life. The deep depression of the situation can make you feel as if God has left us. The purpose of today's lesson is to help you realize that God NEVER leaves you. Even in your darkest times, our Heavenly Dad is sitting in the dark with you. We are often the ones who are so paralyzed by the situation that we don't see him.

Read Isaiah 41:10. Reflect on the verse. If this is God's answer as to what we should do when we feel lost, look at the clues to determine what we must be feeling when we are lost. For example, I will answer the first two, and then let you complete the exercise.

Do not fear – the lost person must be afraid.

For I am with you – the lost person must feel alone.

Do not be dismayed - _____

I am your God - _____

I will strengthen you - _____

I will help you - _____

I will uphold you with my righteous right hand (the right hand is the hand of authority and strength) –

_____

This verse is telling us what we need to do when we feel spiritually lost. The verse tells us to do two things, because God is getting ready to do three things.

Two things for you to do:

1. _____

2. _____

Three things God will do:

1. _____

2. _____

3. _____

So, looking at King David and his situation, do you see where he is allowing God to pull him out of the paralysis of being spiritually lost?

In Psalm 3:3, what does King David loose when he reminds himself that God is his shield? Remember, a shield provides faith, protection, refuge, and salvation. It is a conceptual answer, not black and white. If God is David's Shield, what will he lose?

_____

If God is David's shield, is there any reason to fear? No!

Finally, look at Psalm 3:4. God says in the Isaiah verse that he will strengthen us, help us, and uphold us (with authority and strength). Do you see in verse four how God gave King David strength and help when David cried out and God answered him? _____

I know that most of us, if not all, have experienced a David Moment that left us feeling physically and/or spiritually lost. What we have in today's study verses is God-given hope. We know that God loves us and is waiting with open arms, even when we choose to go in another direction and, for a moment, get physically lost. The Creator of Hope is also there when a situation has left us paralyzed and alone in the dark, and we become spiritually lost. God will never leave you, but He will also not yank you out of the pit of despair. He is sitting there patiently, waiting for you to take His hand and ask Him to help you out of the hole. When we lose hope, we lose sight of the Author and Perfecter of Hope. Two months ago, my mother was diagnosed with breast cancer. We developed a family saying, "God's got this!" That saying was attached to every social media picture, every thought, and yes, every hope. Many miraculous things have happened since her diagnosis, one of which is her healing, but the beauty is, the entire family kept their eyes on God. When you let go of worry and fear, and look into the eyes of the Creator of Hope, you have the God-given confidence to accomplish or overcome anything He puts in front of you.

There is a battle being waged right on your doorstep. He wants to give you the confidence, strength, motivation, and power to jump into the fight. The first step is to acknowledge that the battle is His, the fight is already won, and He will establish your steps to bring you victory!

Thoughts in a Foxhole:

Reflect on times in your life when you were physically or spiritually lost. Write down the major points from your experiences and consider what God did to establish your steps and bring you home.

_____

_____

_____

_____

_____

_____

_____

_____

_____

LESSON THREE
SUDDENLY...

How many times has your life gone in a direction you didn't expect it to go, only to discover later that you are thrilled with the path God set in front of you?

My "suddenly" happened in the spring of 1989. My best friend, Alan Fowler, was accompanying me on a road trip to Flagstaff, Arizona. I had started college at NAU four years prior, and had repetitive dreams of my close friends at the school. We were all seniors in college now, and I felt like I had to go back and see them in order for the dreams to stop. My mom didn't feel comfortable with me making the trip alone, and asked if I would take my best friend with me. I was thrilled with the idea of introducing him to my old friends, and we set off on an adventure that would change my life. We took the six hour drive, enjoying each other's company, and looking forward to our long weekend. I did see my friends. The group of us went out for a fun evening of dinner and music. After the evening was over, I remember looking over at Alan and suddenly seeing him differently than I ever had. At the same moment, Alan looked at me and as if we were on a movie set, we each realized there was more to this relationship than we had realized.

This wasn't what I was expecting. My plan was to move to Dallas after graduation, get an advertising job, and live an exciting life in a big city. In the time it took for a bird to chirp, my whole life was turned upside down. I had never seen Alan as anything more than my best friend, but in the blink of an eye, he was so much more. God led me that day to my best friend, and helped me see that he was also my future.

I was a New Age feminist who thought Christians were short-sighted. In the year following my "suddenly," God changed my heart forever. In trying to get Alan to see that my New Age faith was "truth", God used Alan to take the scales off my eyes so that I could see Jesus for the first time in my life. As the song says, "I once was blind but now I see." By the time we got engaged in April 1990, I was a Bible-believing, church choir singing, middle school youth group-leading Christian. Twenty-eight years after my "suddenly," I can't imagine my life without my best friend, or the Lord and Savior that he introduced me to. I'm not an advertising executive living in the big city. I am a Christian woman who writes Bible studies and is the director of a Christian marriage ministry. I live in a small city with my husband, with whom I have had the privilege of raising two children who love the Lord. That is my best legacy. It is a legacy I wouldn't have had without the Lord turning my plan upside down.

In order for you to be ready for battle, you have to expect the unexpected. The word "suddenly" can be found in the Bible forty-two times. With God, it is important to realize that, in order to be at your most alert, you have to be prepared for God to pull the rug out from under you. When He does, it isn't to hurt you, it's to give you a better place to stand.

Join Moses, Isaiah, Joshua, Job, David, Jeremiah, Daniel, Matthew, Mark, Luke, John, and Paul, in learning how to expect the unexpected and appreciate your *"suddenlys."*

The King David Connection:

Suddenly seems like an innocuous word. I've always thought of it as a word that brings more emphasis to a statement. I have to admit I haven't paid too much attention to it in the Bible, until I started studying Scripture to write this study. The first *suddenly* that caught my eye was in Acts 2:2, when God brought people together from all over the world, and *suddenly* a violent wind filled the house and the people in the house were filled with the Holy Spirit, and started speaking in tongues. God planned this important *suddenly*, but the people did not. Acts 2:1 states that the people were all together in one place. They were studying Scripture, and talking about God and the Risen Savior. One minute, they were fellowshipping, and the next moment, their lives would be changed forever. God planned this moment. He called the people that He wanted, to that room. He filled the room with His Holy Spirit, and He knew that filling would overflow to the joyous moment of them speaking in all of the languages in the world, each language represented in the room.

God plans the *"suddenlys"* that will occur in our lives, but we don't know about them yet. Our job as warriors is to learn to expect the unexpected with patience, attention, and trust. We can start the process by looking at the word "suddenly" in Scripture. In reading all forty-two instances, I have learned that we can divide them into four categories. There are *"suddenlys"* which provide the opportunity to see a miracle, display the powerful presence of God, provide important information, and give us protection in battle.

Many of the answers in the study today are not going to be found in one perfect verse. You will need to read the information, get familiar with the story, and think through the content to discover the answer. Don't let yourself fret over this. Pray before you begin and trust the answers you find. Let's explore the four categories of *"suddenlys"*.

<u>Opportunity to see a miracle:</u>

Read Acts 12:1-10.

    In your own words, speculate as to what you believe were Peter's plans for the day. This is one of those times where you can't read a verse to get a definitive answer. If you wish, look back at the last two chapters to get an idea of what he had been doing, to predict what his plans were.

_____

_____

_____

_____

_____

Peter, at this point, was spreading the Gospel full-time, yet trusting God to lead his day and guide his steps. It is safe to say, however, that Peter was not planning on going to prison that day.

What was God's plan for Peter that day?

_____

_____

_____

What blessings took place because Peter was expecting the unexpected?

_____

_____

_____

How did Peter's *suddenly* help him become a better warrior in God's army?

_____

_____

_____

What take-away can you put in your arsenal from this story as you become a warrior?

_____

_____

_____

_____

Displays the powerful presence of God:

Read Acts 9:1-19.

What were Saul's plans for the day?

_____

_____

_____

_____

What was God's plan for Saul that day?

_____

_____

_____

_____

This is one of my favorite scenes in the Bible to imagine seeing firsthand. Put yourself on the road with Saul. Saul is a determined soldier who feels like he alone can make a difference in this crazy cult of Christians, when *suddenly*, Jesus is talking to him, and the full realization of who Jesus is fills his entire being. What thoughts might have been racing through his mind?

_____

_____

_____

_____

How does God display His powerful presence in this passage?

_____

_____

Does Scripture lead us to believe that Saul expected the unexpected? Why or why not?

_____

_____

What blessings took place, because of Paul's *suddenly*?

_____

_____

_____

How did Paul's *suddenly* help him become a better warrior in God's army?

_____

_____

_____

What take-away can you put in your arsenal from this story as you become a warrior?

_____

_____

_____

_____

Provide important information:

Read Luke 24:1-12

What were the women's plans for the day?

_____

_____

_____

_____

_____

What was God's plan for the women that day?

_____

_____

_____

_____

What important information does this passage provide?

_____

_____

Were these women scared, or did they trust the process? Had these women started expecting the unexpected?

_____

_____

What blessings took place based on the women's *suddenly*?

_____

_____

_____

_____

Speculate upon how this experience helped the women become better warriors in God's army?

_____

_____

_____

What take-away can you put in your arsenal from this story as you become a warrior?

_____

_____

_____

_____

Give protection in battle:

Read Joshua 10:1-15

What were Joshua's plans for the day?

_____

_____

_____

_____

_____

What was God's plan for Joshua that day?

_____

_____

_____

How does this passage show that God gave Joshua protection in battle?

_____

_____

Joshua was told by God what to do, and he followed through. He heard God throughout his _suddenly_. With this in mind, was Joshua expecting the unexpected, or was it that he heard God, and therefore, it was not unexpected?

_____

_____

What blessings took place because Joshua was expecting the unexpected?

_____

_____

_____

_____

How did Joshua's *suddenly* help him become a better warrior in God's army?

_____

_____

_____

What take-away can you put in your arsenal from this story as you become a warrior?

_____

_____

_____

When in a battle, you are constantly required to make decisions based upon the unexpected. In order to become warriors, we need to expect the unexpected, and plan for God to be in the middle of every *suddenly*. Ladies, we are on our way. Today, put your lessons into practice and watch for the "*suddenlys*" God will put in your path.

Thoughts in a Foxhole:

Reflect on what the word *suddenly* means to you, in your life. If it has always been an innocuous word, as it was for me before this study, what does it mean to you now? Ask God to show you a *suddenly* moment in your life. How did He use that *suddenly* to help you become a better warrior in His army?

_____

_____

_____

_____

_____

_____

_____

_____

_____

_____

_____

WEEK FOUR
BATTLE PLAN

Consult with the General

If you haven't yet done so, be still with God and ask Him to show you where He was in your David Moment. Record what He tells you.

_____

_____

_____

_____

_____

_____

_____

_____

_____

_____

_____

_____

_____

_____

Your Tactical Plan

Unfortunately, try as we will, our human hearts will tend to plan our own paths, and take control away from the One who created the path. What steps are you going to take in the future to be vigilant of how God is establishing your steps, and to follow His path and plan for your life?

_____

_____

_____

_____

_____

_____

_____

_____

_____

_____

_____

Week Four Review

This week's Discussion Questions:

1. How well can you discern God's voice? How do you distinguish His voice from your own?

2. Do you listen to God and obey Him more like Elijah, or King David. Explain?

3. Have you ever been physically lost? Explain how you felt.

4. During your David Moment, did you hide from God? Did you get lost? Explain.

5. Has there ever been a time when you were afraid and alone, only to discover that God helped you and gave you strength? Tell us about it.

For the next four questions, consider your David Moment, or a *suddenly* that happened in your life.

6. Did you experience a miracle in your *suddenly*?

7. Did you experience the presence of God during your *suddenly*?

8. What information did you gather from your *suddenly*?

9. How will God use your *suddenly* to protect you in battle?

Joining the Battle

I became a Christian at the ripe old age of twenty-three. At this point, that seems young, but at the time I felt like a late comer to the party. Most of my Christian friends had been such since they were young. I truly had to learn a new language, "Christianese". Here are some of the phrases I heard.

"I asked Jesus into my heart".
"I was born again".
"I was saved".
"Greet one another with a hug and a holy kiss".
"God works in mysterious ways, His wonders to perform".
"The Word of the Lord was anointed".
"Mountaintop experience".
"Under attack from the devil".
"A spirit of heaviness".
"On fire for God!"
"Give a testimony".
"Praise report".
"All things work together for good".
"Led by the Spirit".
"Speak the truth in love".
"Let go and let God".
"God's already won the war".

On the surface, these phrases sounded easy enough to decipher, but I continually asked my fiancé questions.

"Okay, I know I prayed the prayer to be a Christian, but practically speaking, what does it mean for Jesus to be in my heart?"
"What's a holy kiss?"
"What happens when something is anointed?"
"Mountaintop experience, huh?"
"Isn't fire bad? Why would I want to be on fire for the Lord?"
"What war has God won?"

I'm sure we both learned a great deal in those early years as a result of my many questions. Because of my early experiences in the church, I've learned to be sensitive to these "Christianese" phrases, and to help new Christians decipher them as I had to, more than thirty years ago.

We are going to break down and decipher what the last phrase in the list really means. God has won the war. Throughout this study, you've been getting prepared to fight in the battlefield. Today, we will talk about the differences between the battle and the war. We will learn the three levels of warfare: the war, the battle, and the soldier. After this week, you will see how your David Moment fits into our battles, and God's victory.

Lesson One: The War is Won
Lesson Two: What Battle?
Lesson Three: Sleeping Soldiers

LESSON ONE
THE WAR IS WON

The tomb is still sealed. Jesus is lying on a stone slab within the tomb, with a cloth wrapped around Him and a handkerchief covering His face. It is dark, musty, and perfectly quiet within the tomb. Suddenly, Jesus takes a deep breath. He is alive! At that precise moment God won the war! The war is the ultimate struggle between good and evil, but it is so much more than that. The war is between the world and heaven, it is between the flesh and the spirit; it is between our striving to live life through our own strength, and choosing to give that life to Christ, asking Him to be in control. When Jesus took that first breath in the tomb, the war was over; evil lost and God won. That victory brought about the opportunity for God to see us through the lens of Jesus' blood. Through that lens, He sees us as forgiven children. Good won. Heaven won. Spirit won, and the life given to Christ won.

As an American, I view war as a patriotic fight between good and evil. Human warfare, however, is messy, and at best, the sides of good and evil are often murky. Which side of the war you are on determines your view of good and evil.

In *Running for My Life: One Lost Boy's Journey from the Killing Fields of Sudan to the Olympic Games* by Lopez Lomong, we see how difficult it can be to determine the side of good.

Lopez was kidnapped by the rebel soldiers of the civil war in the Sudan during a church service at the age of six. He was literally pulled from his mother's arms and taken to a training camp. Conditions at the camp were beyond awful. The boys ranged from age four to sixteen. If they were old enough and strong enough to hold a gun, they were trained as soldiers. If they were younger, they were kept in a hut, as the soldiers waited for them to die. These soldiers were the very men fighting on the side Lopez' parents were supporting in the civil war. These young boys were fed one meal every day, mostly of dirt mixed with corn meal. These boys didn't leave the hut. They toileted, ate, slept, cried, and prayed in the one room hut for months.

Lopez describes three older boys as his three angels, who helped him escape the training death camp. They carried him on their backs when needed, and ran for three days to the safety of a Kenyan Refugee camp. That camp's conditions were not good, but Lopez was far safer within its walls. Once there, he was able to be baptized and to grow in his faith. Eventually, his presence in the camp gave him the opportunity to go to America and prosper, eventually representing the USA in the 2008 and 2012 Olympics.

God never left Lopez' side. The three angels were never seen after that first night in the refugee camp. Whether they were actual angels, or people sent by God to take care of Lopez, we may never know, but God's influence in Lopez' life went far beyond the three angels. Most profound for me, was the fact that Lopez looked for God in everything that happened to him. Instead of focusing on the fact that his favorite day was Tuesday because that was the day the American's trash was disposed of, which they ate from, he thanked God for the occasional banana or scrap of meat God gave him as a gift from the trash.

Later in life, Lopez reminisces upon where he has been:

> "God had brought me so far, through war, through eating garbage and running to forget about my empty stomach. No matter what I went through, God was always with me. He had always had this moment planned for me, both the good times and the bad, from the killing fields of Sudan to these Olympic Games and back again."[1]

For Lopez, as for so many, there wasn't a clear good versus bad side of the civil war in Sudan. But it is clear that God's struggle against evil won that battle. God cared for, influenced, and made a difference through, the almost unbelievable faith and life of a small six-year-old boy from a village in Sudan.[1]

Today, we will explore the war that God has declared won. The story of this young boy, Lopez, proves that God is in control, and that what Satan means for evil, God can and will turn on its toes to become good.

The King David Connection:

Read Isaiah 14:12-15

Isaiah, talking about Satan, tells of the beginning of the war. Why did the war begin?

_____

_____

_____

_____

Read 2 Corinthians 4:1-6

So, Satan is the "god of this world". What do you think this means?

_____

_____

_____

_____

Satan is allowed to wreak havoc on the Earth. What does it mean to "blind the mind of unbelievers"?

_____

_____

_____

_____

How is Satan still creating havoc on the Earth? Give examples.

_____

_____

_____

_____

Read Romans 6:8-11 and 23

Through these verses, we understand why Jesus' resurrection won the war. Verse nine states, "Christ, having been raised from the dead, is never to die again; death no longer is master over Him."(NASB) What or who is "death?"

_____

In verse ten, what died, once and for all?

_____

If sin died once and for all, can Satan's havoc actually cause eternal damage to the good that is Christ? _____. Let me be clear, Satan's havoc can create problems in our lives, but when Jesus died and rose again, the grace that God gave us killed the power sin had in our lives. God cannot be in the presence of sin, but the moment Jesus rose again, we were freed from the bondage that sin holds. If we believe that Jesus died on the cross and rose again, and we profess our sin to Him, then God the Father sees us through the lens of His son, Jesus. When Jesus rose from the dead, evil _____, good _____ and God won the _____.

Praise God! Evil <u>lost</u>, good <u>won,</u> and God won the <u>war</u>.

When we make a decision to believe in Christ, and give our lives to Him, what is lost?

_____

If death is lost, what is won?

_____

What is the free gift of God, as referred to in verse twenty-three?

_____

Read 1 John 4:2-4.

Look closely at verse four. Who are the little children?

_____

It says the little children have "overcome them". Who is them? _____

What does it mean to "overcome them"?

_____

_____

What do you need to do to "overcome them"?

_____

Because we are the children of God, we need to do nothing. Why?

_____

_____

The war began when Satan aspired to be equal to God. Ever since, Satan has tried to influence the world through sin. Our Heavenly Father cannot be surrounded by sin, making it impossible for us sinful humans to live with Him in eternity. When Jesus, the perfect lamb, was crucified, and rose again three days later, the bondage of sin was broken. No longer did we have to strive to be perfect. From that moment, the people of the Earth had a choice. If we understand that Christ died for the forgiveness of our sin, our sins are forgiven. If we give Jesus our life, He will always be with us, near us, and in control. At that moment, our sin is as far as the east is from the west. Essentially, the choice is ours. We can accept the gift that Jesus gave us on the cross and spend eternity in heaven. The war is over, God won.

Satan created a playground of evil during the civil war in Sudan, but God, through Lopez Lomong, brought about a better life for countless people. Lopez saw, felt, and heard God during that awful time. After competing in the Beijing Olympics, Lopez had the world's attention, and as such, was able to care for hundreds of thousands of people in his home country. Evil was defeated and glory was given to God. The war really is won! God is in control. He is in control in your life, as well as in Lopez'. Put your sword at His feet and bask in His peace.

Thoughts in a Foxhole:

Reflecting on your David Moment, what did Satan mean for evil?

_____

_____

_____

_____

_____

_____

_____

_____

How did God turn your David Moment into something good? If you are just now starting to see the good He is in the process of doing, record the details below:

_____

_____

_____

_____

_____

_____

_____

_____

_____

LESSON TWO
WHAT BATTLE?

If the war is won, why do I have to fight? There are countless battles throughout a day in the life of a Christian. It is Satan's goal to destroy God's influence in our lives, as well as God's influence in other's lives through us (our witness). Satan knows his power is limited. It is through these battles that he gains the few advantages he has.

In researching this week of lessons, I talked to several members of the United States Military. I asked them a simple, yet often confusing, question: "If you knew the war was won before you stepped on the battlefield, would it change the way you fought?" A member of the Combined Joint Special Operations Air Component (CJSOAC) answered my question in a way I wasn't expecting.

> "I don't think it would change how I fought. I may know that we would win the war, but at what cost? When we went out on the battlefield, I never questioned whether we would win or not. I took comfort in the skills and professionalism of those around me. I was confident in the team's ability to meet any challenge. It never affected the effort I put into my particular job because those around me depended on me to do my job well. We did it for each other and to make sure each of us came home at the end of the battle. Winning meant coming home together. So we always did our best to make sure the person next to us came home even though we were confident we would win the battle."[2]

Oh my sweet sister, THIS is our battle. Our battle is to get all of us home in heaven. The war is won, but the day-to-day battles are yet to be fought and won. We have to hone our skills, and be ready to do what it takes, through knowledge and trust in our Savior, to bring everyone home with us.

Ladies, we are Warriors. Pick up your shield, and let's battle together, bringing our friends, family, and loved ones home with us. Those around you are depending on you. My sister Warriors, let's take a closer look at the battles we need to fight and how God already gave us the means to win.

The King David Connection

When I think of a battle, I often picture two opponents facing each other with their fists at the ready, prepared to strike. This is not what it looks like when we battle Satan. Satan has learned to be tricky. He can scheme, lie, and tempt you into fulfilling his desires. In fact, one of Satan's most successful schemes throughout the ages has been manipulating people into believing that he doesn't exist. If he doesn't exist, people are free to do what they want. In this scenario, there is no sin, and therefore, no consequences of that sin. There is life on Earth, and when life is over, it is over, so hakuna matata and Carpe Diem. Unfortunately, Satan does exist, and we battle him every day.

Our battle can be in the morning, when we are too tired for our quiet time, or it can be in that non-Christian friend we gossip with, or in the doubt Satan whispers in our ear.

Battles vary in size, complexity, and theme, but they all fall into the limited power which Satan holds. Fortunately, our Heavenly Dad is far more powerful than the author of lies. Let's look at two different types of battles, and see how to fight.

Satan desires to destroy God's influence in our life:

Read Ephesians 6:12-18

What does this verse say we are fighting?

_____

_____

_____

Put your answer above into your own words. What are we fighting?

_____

Re-read verse thirteen. Why are we putting on the armor of God?

_____

_____

God gives us protection from our enemy, and weapons to fight. Praise God! Paying close attention to verses 14-18, match the soldier's armor with the godly attribute it represents by drawing a line from the armor to its attribute.

Gird your loins   Preparation of the Gospel of Peace
Breastplate   Salvation
Shod your feet   Righteousness
Shield   Faith
Helmet   Spirit/Word of God
Sword   Truth

Warriors, we are not done with this verse yet. We are leaving this lesson today, readied for battle. In the spaces below, write one example (for each) of how you will use that piece of equipment to destroy Satan's influence in your life and build God's influence.

Girded Loins:

_____

_____

Breastplate:

_____

_____

Shod: Feet

_____

_____

Shield:

_____

_____

Helmet:

_____

_____

Sword:

_____

_____

Prayer (one of most important weapons, but one that doesn't have a piece of armor connected):

_____

_____

Satan desires to destroy God's influence in other's lives through us:

In the introduction of this lesson, we heard from a member of the CJSOAC. He helped us see that, as Christians, just as with military members, our goal is to bring all of God's children home. There are many ways in which we can be God's warriors in that mission; communicating the Gospel, being compassionate to others, giving grace, and offering forgiveness, just to name a few. But sisters, this is the Great Commission; this is where we share the gospel.

Read the verses below. They all give us responsibility in relation to unbelievers. Read each and write down the main responsibility that verse is asking of us concerning those who haven't met our Savior.

1 Peter 3:15:

_____

Matthew 5:16

_____

2 Corinthians 5:20

_____

Matthew 28:16-20

_____

I know that, at first glance, each of these verses look different, but look closely. Each of them is asking us to realize that when we are seen by unbelievers, they are looking at the reflection of Jesus. Ladies, this is our mission. This is what we are called to do. In the space below write, in your own words, the common thing these verses are asking of us.

_____

_____

We have the privilege of being asked to be Christ-like in our lives.

Read Colossians 4:2-6. These verses specifically ask us to do four things with unbelievers. See if you can find each and write them in the space below.

1. _____

2. _____

3. _____

4. _____

Ladies, I am so proud of you, and confident in your ability to go onto the battlefield and show Christ to the world. Have you put it together? You just spent an hour studying the Bible in order to learn that, to be successful in the many battles that you will face in life, we need to do three things:

1. Trust our Lord and Savior in the battle.
2. Become friends with the Savior of the World, while learning from Him.
3. Be Christ's reflection.

Today, you will finish this lesson and be in battle. Before this study, you may not have even realized that you were living your life on the battlefield, but now, not only are you aware of it, you are prepared for it. Go out there, use your David Moment to see how God has been involved in your life, and holding your hand throughout. Show others the loving, living God of the Bible. Fight battles and win. You are the child of the Creator and Savior of the Universe. You will battle today, and Satan's power is limited. Hold Jesus' hand and win the battles He allows you to face. He's there.

Thoughts in a Foxhole:

Think through the many different ways that God can use your David Moment to build His influence in your life, and then also in the lives of others through you. List the ideas you come up with below.

Building God's influence in my life:

_____

_____

_____

_____

_____

_____

_____

_____

Building God's influence in other's lives through me (His witness). Be sure to include ideas on sharing the Gospel:

_____

_____

_____

_____

_____

_____

With whom is God leading you to share the Gospel?

_____

_____

_____

_____

LESSON THREE
UNLIKELY WARRIORS

After "Chicago," I slowly but surely realized that I was a warrior, and that God had been preparing me for battle for quite some time. My first thought after that realization was, "Oh no, God, you don't know who you are dealing with here. I like to please people; I seem to find things to worry about, and courage isn't part of my daily routine." After what I'm sure was a short chuckle from Jesus, He reminded me, through Philippians 4:13, that the mud He had allowed me to walk through had helped me learn to trust Him. It is this faith that makes me ready for battle, not anything I can do, or have done, myself. I, like you, am an unlikely warrior. Do you feel unworthy of this title? That's okay. I do, too, and history is full of people that God has used powerfully who didn't feel capable.

Have you ever heard of Edward Kimball? Mr. Kimball was also an unlikely warrior. He was a Sunday School teacher with a class full of teenage boys. He desperately wanted to reach these boys for Jesus, but felt like it was an impossible task. He explained later in his life that working with these boys was similar to herding cats. Each of these boys had things to do other than be in church. Getting them to pay attention and treat their faith as anything more than another academic pursuit desired and expected by their parents, was difficult. Mr. Kimball kept pursuing the boys. He studied the boys, and their desires. He worked at different ways to reach them and finally decided to talk to them one-by-one.

His desire to reach the boys individually, led him to a shoe store in Detroit. Mr. Kimball went to the back stockroom, where one of his young students was working. He told the boy that he was afraid for him, and would like to talk to him. The boy came down from his ladder and the two went to the basement and talked. At the end of the meeting, the young D.L. Moody accepted Christ.

Yes, Mr. Moody went on to reach over 100 million people on multiple continents, but God's spiritual dominoes don't end there.

Dwight L. Moody led J. Wilbur Chapman to Christ
J. Wilbur Chapman led Billy Sunday to Christ
Billy Sunday led Mordecai Ham to Christ
Mordecai Ham led Billy Graham to Christ

Many people say that Billy Graham reached more people for Christ than any other person in history. So, looking back, a teacher, who desperately wanted to reach the teenage boys in his Sunday School class, was a warrior for Christ. Through his obedience, Edward Kimball facilitated more people hearing about Jesus than anyone ever.

Sisters, I know that I am an Unlikely Warrior, but so are you, and so was Edward Kimball. We need not concern ourselves with our talents, or even our difficulties. We need to keep trusting Jesus and looking to Him for guidance. He will set up the spiritual dominoes and make the pieces fall into place. Oh, how I desire to be one of His game pieces. Let's look at a few of the Bible's Unlikely Warriors, and see what we can glean from this awesome job.

The King David Connection

We need to engage in hand-to-hand combat in each battle we are involved in. Although God will request different things from each of us, our responsibility in the war is simple: be in the Word, listen to God, and respond accordingly. I am excited to share with you the stories of some of God's Unlikely Warriors. Today, I am only highlighting women, but the Bible is full of people who never thought of themselves as warriors, but were used powerfully by our living God. I love the stories of these women. We are only going to glance at their stories, but any of these stories could be an entire Bible study of its own. I would like you to put yourself in their stories. You might relate to some of these women better than others; however, each was brave and each was used powerfully by God. Just how, we will soon discover.

Rahab

Read Joshua 2:1-16

How did God use Rahab powerfully?

_____

_____

_____

_____

_____

Describe her God-given gift in one word. _____

What was God able to do because of her?

_____

_____

_____

_____

Jael

Read Judges 4

How did God use Jael powerfully?

_____

_____

_____

_____

_____

Describe her God-given gift in one word. _____

What was God able to do because of her?

_____

_____

_____

_____

Hannah

Read 1 Samuel 1

How did God use Hannah powerfully?

_____

_____

_____

_____

_____

Describe her God-given gift in one word. _____

What was God able to do because of her? Samuel was pivotal in Israel's history. To discover more of Samuel's life, you can read Acts 13:20, Psalm 99:6-7, and Jeremiah 15:1.

_____

_____

_____

_____

Lois and Eunice

Read 2 Timothy 1:1-5

How did God use Lois and Eunice powerfully?

_____

_____

_____

_____

_____

Describe their God-given gifts in one word. _____

What was God able to do because of Lois and Eunice? If you would like to learn more about Timothy's role in the early church, read 1 Timothy 1:1-7

_____

_____

_____

_____

The woman at the well

Read John 4:1-30 and 39-42

How did God use the woman at the well powerfully?

_____

_____

_____

_____

_____

Describe her God-given gift in one word. _____

What was God able to do because of her?

_____

_____

_____

_____

Ladies, let's think through what we have learned, and connect these Unlikely Warriors to King David. We know that David was a warrior for God, but his beginnings were humble. When David was a young boy, neither he, nor his family, could have ever imagined the way God would use him powerfully. Are you starting to see? We should never allow ourselves to limit God through our doubts in our own abilities. We ARE warriors, chosen by God. Yes, we are limited, but God is not. He can, and will, use us.

We have to stop worrying about how God will use us powerfully, and rest in the fact that He will. Through some of us, God will reach thousands at one time in a stadium, but others of us will be used powerfully, by facing depression and taking a step out of the house when everything in us is screaming to stay in the comfort and security of home. Don't count yourself as unworthy, because in so doing, you are unintentionally limiting the influence you allow God to have in your life. Trust Him. Listen to Him. Have faith in His ability to use you, because He will. You are His Warrior.

Thoughts in a Foxhole:

Think through the ways that God might be using you right now. Keep in mind, God's children sometimes get talents and gifts confused. You may have a talent for something that He is not using for His glory. In the same way, He may be using you powerfully right now in a way you never thought you were talented. Use the space below to brainstorm the ways in which He might be using you. When do people listen to you? What do people see in you as brave? What do people admire about you that can be used for His glory? Keep your David Moment in mind; He is probably using that to propel you.

_____

_____

_____

_____

_____

Week Five
Battle Plan

Consult with the General

Talk to our General, and ask Him to point out the area, or areas, He would like you to focus on to bring glory to Him. Where is He calling you to use your gifts powerfully? Remember, our goal is to bring as many of God's children home with us as possible. How do you feel He is going to use you, an unlikely Warrior, to bring His children home? You can be more general here. We will be more specific in your Tactical Plan.

_____

_____

_____

_____

_____

_____

_____

_____

_____

_____

_____

Your Tactical Plan

Using the information you learned above, write down one thing that you will start doing today to bring His children home and for His glory. This is your opportunity to be specific. Remember, it is our privilege as Warriors of Christ to share the Gospel, and to use our spiritual gifts powerfully for His Glory. How are you going to do that?

_____

_____

_____

_____

_____

_____

_____

_____

_____

_____

_____

Week Five Review

This week, it is important that we understand the three different levels of warfare. We learned what it means to win the war, and we learned why we still need to fight, even though the war is won. We also learned what our daily battles look like, and how our goal is to bring God's children home with us while also bringing glory to God. Finally, we got to see some of the many Unlikely Warriors in the Bible, and how we, like them, can be used powerfully by our General and Heavenly Dad.

My sweet sisters in Christ, we need to fully understand that the women of the Bible were not wilting flowers. The women of the Bible were warriors alongside their make brothers in Christ, and so are we. God gave us gifts that He does, and will, use for His glory. The female warriors of the Bible were fierce sisters-in-Christ who made a difference in the Kingdom of God, and SO ARE YOU!

This week's Discussion Questions:

1. Have you seen how Satan has tried to create havoc in your life, yet God won? Please share.

2. How did your decision to choose life through Christ give you freedom from the war?

3. Where do you see God in control of your life?

4. What piece of armor are you using the most, right now, for His glory? Tell us about that.

5. Tell us about the last time you went to battle for an unbeliever.

6. Which Unlikely Warrior from the text do you identify with the most? Why?

7. Are you starting to see yourself as a warrior? If so, how is He using you? If not, can you see it in the near future?

8. How is God using your David Moment to create the warrior within you?

WEEK SIX

Being Fierce

In Georgia, Angela Cavallo lifted a 3000 lb Chevy Impala off of her son and held it for five minutes until neighbors came and pulled her son to safety.[1]

In Florida, Joseph Welch came to his son's rescue when an alligator clamped down on his son's arm. He punched and kicked the alligator until it released his son.[2]

In 1988, on the set of the TV show Magnum PI, a helicopter careened out of control, pinning a man underwater. Instantly, a local Hawaiian, Warren "Tiny" Everal, lifted the 1,150 pound helicopter off of the trapped man.[3]

In New Mexico, a woman runs alongside a driverless, moving school bus filled with kids. While running, she is able to get the kids to open the door. She climbs onto the school bus, moves the collapsed driver, takes control of the bus, and stops it before any children or bystanders are hurt.[4]

These people were fierce. They had a job to do, and were not going to let circumstances, fear, or worry get in their way. This week, we are going to become fierce, even though, for a while, I was apprehensive to use that word. When I looked up the definition of fierce, I found synonyms like wild, savage, forceful, and hostile. The definition is "furiously eager, or intense". At first, I shied away from this definition and started trying to think of another, more appropriate word. I studied several words, yet kept coming back to "fierce". After praying about it, it occurred to me; there is nothing wrong with Christian women being wild, savage, forceful, and even hostile for Christ. Women of the Bible were quite fierce. Many gave everything for Christ. Mary willingly subjected herself to public ridicule, and was an eyewitness to her beloved son's brutal death. Ruth lost her husband, then left everything she knew, to take care of her mother-in-law. In the process, she found the living God, and became the great-grandmother of King David, and featured prominently in the lineage of Jesus Christ. The Samaritan woman at the well went from an outcast, to one of the first mass evangelists for Christ. Esther risked her life to save the lives of her people, showing us that breaking the intimidation of others can bring glory to God. For goodness' sake, Jael helped save the Israelites by driving a tent peg into the temple of Sisera, the Canaanite general of King Jabin.

Women of the Bible didn't simply sit at home, weaving baskets and cooking meals. They were on the front lines of the greatest battle the world has ever, or will ever, experience. Sister, you are a Warrior alongside these amazing ladies. Drop your worry and fear, and pick up your sword. We have a battle to fight.

This week's lessons are designed to help us become fierce Warriors. As Warriors of the living God, we are called to do what is necessary to do His will and bring the children of God home. Let's drop our insecurities and follow Mary, the Samaritan woman, Ruth, and Esther, and be fierce!

Day 1: Fierce Forgiveness
Day 2: Soldier Keep Movin'
Day 3: Victory!
Conclusion: Charge!

LESSON ONE
FIERCE FORGIVENESS

After somehow getting to her bedroom, Michelle sat on her bed, with her phone in her hand. She was ready to call her family and go home. At the young age of twenty-three, she knew her health was failing her. She didn't have enough food to eat, and she didn't have the support system she now knew she needed. There was only one thing to do; she needed to trust Jesus and go home. In the past four years, she had survived a human trafficking situation and a recent attack; yet she felt more peace than she had ever felt in her life. Five minutes before she had somehow gotten to her room and locked her door, she had experienced the worst event of her life. She describes the situation as if evil filled the room and then, as quickly as evil entered, love came crashing into the darkness.

She explains, "I felt a love and a peace that is indescribable. I knew that the only answer as to the source of that compassion, love, and forgiveness was Jesus. Although the horrific event continued around me, I felt the peace of God fill the room. Forgiveness for others, as well as myself, flooded my soul, and as quickly as evil entered, Christ took over." Even though the following year carried with it a cancer diagnosis and the need to start life over, the peace continued. "My past couldn't imprison me any longer, nor could the cancer diagnosis. Jesus had forgiven me; I had forgiven the people who had hurt me, and I was truly free."[5]

Graceli Veson endured years of pain from people who were supposed to love her. She was hurt, ignored, and not believed. Once the truth came out, she was told that she had to stay quiet, in order to keep her loved ones safe. At the age of twelve, she pushed the hurt to a place that she thought she could ignore. She explains that it wasn't until she was twenty-three, when a friend got a hold of her, and explained forgiveness, that she realized that the "pushing the hurt aside" wasn't forgiveness.

"My friend explained that the only way I could truly take away the pain from my past was to push it to the forefront and forgive. At first I thought she was crazy, but eventually I listened. Eleven years after the hurt, I forgave the people who had hurt me. For the first time in my life, I was able to feel free and unburdened by my past. I now understood that forgiveness doesn't excuse the act, but it frees me from having to endure it any longer."[6]

A famous forgiveness speaker, and beloved Christian, Corrie ten Boom, came face-to-face with her own forgiveness story, when a Nazi concentration camp guard came up to her after one of her speaking opportunities in post-World War II Germany. The guard, who had recently given his life to Jesus, didn't recognize Ms. Ten Boom, but she could never forget him. This man, who was responsible for the death of her family and countless others, came up to Corrie with his arm outstretched, asking for her forgiveness as a concentration camp survivor. She explains that his hand must have only been hanging in the air for mere seconds, but to her, it felt like hours. In that time, she had to wrestle with one of the most difficult decisions of her life. As she mechanically obeyed what she knew she had to do, her hand grasped his, and a miraculous thing happened. At the moment that their hands touched, her Savior supplied the feeling, and forgiveness flooded her soul.[7]

These stories of forgiveness are dramatic. You may be like me, and have never had to endure pain such as this, but you undoubtedly have had a hurt in your life that you have had to forgive. I, too, have been hurt. It wasn't until I forgave that the situation was truly in my past.

Sisters, forgiveness is the key to the prison doors that we allow ourselves to be hidden behind. Forgiveness strengthens the most important muscle we will use in our battle – the heart. In order to win the battle we cannot harbor hate, bitterness or hurt in our hearts; we must allow our Heavenly Dad to cleanse our souls, in order to be battle ready.

Michelle, Graceli Veson, Corrie ten Boom, King David, Stephen, and many other Warriors, have taken this important step. Now it is your turn.

We are honored to be given the awesome responsibility to be Jesus' soldiers, so let's do what is necessary to have the full power and strength of Christ behind every step we take.

The King David Connection:

We are going to look at two important Warriors, and see how they not only forgave in the midst of extreme hurt, but ultimately won their battle, because they were able to forgive those who persecuted them. Since this is the King David Connection, we will first look at David.

Write Psalm 3:8 in the space below and highlight, or underline, where David forgives those hurting him.

_____

_____

_____

_____

_____

The second half of verse eight says "May your blessing be on your people". (NIV) Who is the text referring to? Read Isaiah 43:1-3. You probably already know who God's people are, but read this beautiful verse to put it into perspective. Not only does it solidify who God's chosen people are, it says two more important things.

Who are God's people? _____

In verses 2-3, what two things will God always do for His people?

1. _____
   _____

2. _____
   _____

Isaiah clearly says that God will always be with His people, and will protect His people. When King David asked for God to bless His people, he wasn't only asking God to forgive them, he was asking God to give abundantly to them. I think it is important to keep in mind that David wasn't asking God to give him back the kingdom, he was asking God to do what was best for Israel. Please keep in mind when King David is asking for this blessing.

When King David asks for blessing to be given to Israel, is he safe yet? _____

Is King David still in the cave, afraid for his life? _____

Are the people of Israel still hunting David; trying to kill him? _____

When does this story suggest that we should forgive others? Do we forgive after the hurt, when we've had the opportunity to justify why the person may have hurt us, or in the midst of the hurt?

_____

Did King David wait to forgive until the people hunting him asked for forgiveness? _____

Extrapolate with your knowledge of the situation; how did King David's forgiveness affect Israel?

_____

_____

_____

_____

Now, let's look at another one of God's Warriors: Stephen. Stephen was one of the gentle giants of the New Testament. The church was growing by leaps and bounds. Peter's speech to the crowd of Jews had reached approximately three thousand people at once. The apostles were being overrun with requests for help from new believers. They soon decided that they needed to have a group of seven men who were full of the spirit, and wisdom, to help fulfill this need so that they could do what they were called to do, which was pray and teach (Acts 6:3-5). Stephen was specifically mentioned as one of those men. In fact, his work in that area is so well known that many churches today have Stephen's Ministries, which help parishioners. It was during this time that Stephen was arrested and hence gave a propelling speech, which academically put the Sanhedrin in its place (Acts 7). Stephen said, among other things, that God did not reside solely in their temple. He also, in verse 53 said, "you who received the law as delivered by angels and did not keep it." (ESV) This speech angered the Sanhedrin greatly. As if this wasn't enough, Stephen was led by the Holy Spirit to gaze into the heavens. When he did, the heavens opened, and he reported to the group what he was allowed to see, "The Son of Man standing at the right hand of God." At this, they took him out to be stoned. Read Acts 7:54-60. In what verse does Stephen forgive those stoning him?

_____

Was Stephen safe when he asked God to forgive those who were stoning him? _____

Does Stephen get out of this ordeal alive? _____

When does this story suggest we should forgive others? Do we forgive during the hurt, or after we wait and see what happened? _____

Did Stephen wait to forgive until those stoning him had asked for forgiveness? _____

One of the outcomes here is specifically written. Who witnessed this stoning in verse fifty-eight?

_____

_____

Read Acts 22:20. Did Saul (now Paul) approve of Stephen's murder? _____

Read Acts 9:15. What did this witness of Stephen's murder go on to do?

_____

_____

_____

It is my contention that Stephen's murder affected Saul for evil at the time, but then affected him differently after his conversion. Extrapolate with your knowledge of the situation. How did Stephen's forgiveness and murder affect Paul the apostle?

_____

_____

_____

_____

We have taken a lot of time to explore what it means to forgive, but what if you are the one who needs forgiveness? I think we are quick to want the bad feelings associated with sin to go away. Some of us ask forgiveness very quickly, in order to alleviate the consequence and guilt of sin. That quick response to sin is not wrong, but it is also not wrong to allow our feeling to marinate on what we did. Ask for forgiveness quickly and honestly. If forgiveness is not given, you have still obeyed God. The sin is finished, but the feeling of wrongdoing may persist. Even if forgiveness is granted, those feelings can remain. If they do, follow it. Pray about it. Is there a lesson God wants you to learn from it? Rest in the fact that, if you asked for forgiveness, you have done what your heavenly Dad asked of you. But don't be in such a hurry to move on. Sit there a while, and glean what you can from the situation. However, it is important to note that we need to prayerfully know <u>when</u> to move on, and stop bashing ourselves for past mistakes. When we are forgiven by God, those sins are removed, as far as the east is from the west.

Before we leave this lesson, it is important to practically understand how to grant forgiveness. This is a lesson that I did not understand for years. Once I did, it has become one of my favorite subjects to teach. In order to forgive, do what King David, Stephen, and Jesus Christ did: speak it out loud. I think it's important to verbalize the act. Then, do not bring it up again. It is done. Gone. As far as the east is from the west. I know that there are some horrible things that have happened to people. Forgiveness does not make light of the wrong. Forgiveness does not alleviate the consequences of that wrong. It simply frees you from the burden of the wrong. You are no longer responsible for anything associated with what happened. You are free, and you are ready for battle.

Ladies, let's get ready for the battle of our lives, and get rid of the burdens of resentment and bitterness. For some, this will be easy. For others, this might be the most difficult lesson in this entire study. Either way, it is time, Warriors! God is waiting on the other side of forgiveness with the warm blanket of love, strength, and power. Grab it, Ladies!

Thoughts in a Foxhole:

This is your opportunity to reflect on your life. Is there anyone you need forgive? Is there anyone of whom you need to ask forgiveness? Take an inventory of your life. I have worked with people who come to me because they are angry with a current situation, only to find that there is something larger in their past that was not forgiven. Forgiveness is important. Ask Jesus to reveal to you those He knows you need to forgive, or ask forgiveness from.

People I need to forgive:

_____

_____

_____

_____

_____

People I need to seek forgiveness from:

_____

_____

_____

_____

_____

_____

It is vital that, when talking about forgiveness, we not only plan for it, we do it. You don't need to think about it, or formulate it, or decide your next move. You simply need to go down the list of people which God gave you above, and check them off as you forgive each one, out loud, with obedience in your heart. You do not need to wait for the emotional acceptance to catch up with your situation. You need to, once and for all, forever forgive.

Check the box when done.

Lesson Two
Soldier Keep Movin'

It was 1966, in the Quang Ngai Province of North Vietnam. I was with the point platoon that was assigned to dispatch, or destroy, the outpost of an NVA (North Vietnam Aggressor) battalion. That means I was with the first group to see fighting on the front line.

In order to understand the battle we experienced, it helps to understand what the natural landscape of the province looked like. There were areas of dense jungle forests. The trees were so tightly packed together that you couldn't see people five feet inside. Every few acres, the forest cleared to an open patch of land. That is exactly where this battle took place.

The fighting started at the top of the ridge, but soon slid down the embankment to a large, open rice patty. In mere moments of reaching the space below, the tree line adjacent to the rice patty exploded with gun fire. We were sitting ducks to the one hundred NVA troops hiding in the trees with automatic rifles. Within seconds, our troops were decimated.

Suddenly, I heard a faint cry for help. I looked around and saw, twenty feet away, in the open field, a friend and fellow marine who had been hit.

Those twenty feet may not seem like much, but in the midst of battle, it might as well have been the next town over. Gunfire was spattering the field like the rays of the sun hitting you on a hot day. I was the medic, this was my job, and he was my friend, so I fell on my belly and crawled over to my friend. I reach him and tended to his wounds. As I did, I felt a searing pain explode in the palm of my hand. I looked over and noticed that I'd been hit, but I knew that I couldn't worry about that now. The pain had to wait. This was my job; I needed to help these soldiers. I pulled my friend to a relatively safe place and started to examine my hand, but I heard "Corpsman", echo across the field from numerous locations. As I crawled through the rice field, the fighting, and the dead, I collected ammunition from those soldiers who no longer needed it. I had to get to the next marine that needed my help. I reached him, tended to his wounds, and pulled him to the safest place I could find. As I turned toward the ever-present call for "Corpsman", I felt my knee explode with pain. I could not look. I knew I didn't need my knee to crawl. I had to get to the next marine. As I reached the next marine and pulled him to safety, I realized I'd been hit in the thigh. It was OK, it only hurt when I concentrated on it, "keep moving, soldier", was all I kept repeating to myself. In the midst of helping the next marine, I was hit in the shoulder. Now I was starting to feel it. I was close to the embankment, and was heading toward safety, when I heard a faint call for "Corpsman."

I looked at the bullet-ridden field, and said to myself, "keep moving, soldier. This is your job. The pain can wait. I need to help these soldiers." I lifted my head, turned toward the fighting, and once more, with the resolute attitude to save my friend, crawled out onto the field. I pulled him to the embankment and, as I was dressing his wounds, I felt the fourth shot, a wound I could not ignore.

This story, adapted from historical facts, is that of Robert R. Ingram. As a result of this encounter, he received the Congressional Medal of Honor, the Silver Star, and the Purple Heart. Just as Robert Ingram, when in the midst of battle, lift your head, turn toward the fighting, and resolutely decide what you will do. You don't know whom you will pull to safety..[8]

Sisters, we are inching our way toward the end of this study. This chapter brings everything we've learned into focus. In our battle, there will be trouble, but we have to decide to keep our eyes glued on the One who has won the war. We must have faith, stop worrying, be courageous, forgive, and keep moving. Along the way, we don't know who we will be given the honor to pull to safety. Through the power of Jesus Christ, the one saved might even be you.

The King David Connection:

Ladies, if we look at our wounds and the battle in front of us, we can get lost in the pain, hurt, and anguish of the fighting. Look up into the eyes of the One who is faithful, the One who cares, and the One who is good. In those eyes lie peace, comfort, and love beyond understanding. He doesn't require anything more from you than your faith that He will see you through the hurt. So, do you know what that means? Through the supernatural ability of our Savior, keep moving. Put one step in front of the other.

We are going to look at King David, who had to do just that. Let's see what we can learn from his story.

Read Psalm 3:4-5. Describe the emotions King David was experiencing in verse four.

_____

_____

In verse five, King David slept. Although this is the shortest verse in the psalm, it is loaded with information. What did King David do? _____

What does sleeping require? _____

    King David, up to this point, had been anguishing on the problem at hand. In verse four, King David has an emotional transformation. Verse three hints that he finally looked up into the eyes of Jesus, and felt enough peace to sleep for the first time in, possibly, weeks.

What can we learn about moving forward during pain? What is the result of the obedience required to keep moving?

_____

Let's continue with King David. King David's troops have won the battle over Absalom and his men. In so doing, the king's son, Absalom, has been killed. King David is beside himself with grief. In the midst of the grief, Joab, one of his most trusted advisors, gets upset with him.

Read 2 Samuel 19:1-8

How does Joab tell King David to keep moving?

_____

_____

_____

_____

_____

_____

How did King David respond?

_____

_____

Did King David magically feel like celebrating? _____

What can we learn from this story about moving forward while in the midst of pain?

_____

_____

So often, we want to make sense of our David Moment. We want to understand why we are going through it. I can't tell you the number of times that I've looked at my own situation, and examined it in hopes that I figure out what I'm supposed to learn so that I can learn it quicker.

Read John 16:33. What does this verse assure us that we will experience in this world?

_____

Fill in the missing word from John 16:33:

"These things I have spoken to you, so that in Me you may have peace. In the world you have tribulation, but take courage; I have _____ the world."

What does it mean to overcome the world?

_____

_____

_____

It is important to note that there are false teachers in the world who will tell you that, if you follow God's will, He will bless you and make your life trouble-free. There are other false teachers who preach that God wants to eliminate trouble, so that you remain happy in life. Sisters, please do not believe either of these. It is true that God does not cause evil to occur in your life, but He will allow unpleasant things to happen. So, what do we do when God makes some mountains unmovable? We praise Him. I have seen this firsthand with my own David Moment. It is important to separate our love for what God does, from the reason for praising Him. We can praise Him for what He does, but we first need to praise Him for Who He is. God is faithful, He is good, and He loves us.

Let's look one more time at King David's experience.

How did God show His <u>faithfulness</u> to King David?

_____

_____

How did God show His <u>goodness</u> to King David?

_____

_____

How did God show His <u>love</u> to King David?

_____

_____

I am so proud of you for completing this study. This one was especially difficult for me. I know Jesus tells us that there will be trouble in our lives, but I always tend to think (if I were extremely honest) that I will be the one exception.

Ladies, when we are experiencing tribulation, we have a powerful weapon that the Holy Spirit provides: our attitude. We have the choice to find joy, we have the choice to praise, and we have the choice to be thankful. As Philippians 4:6-7 says, "Do not be anxious about anything, but in every situation, by prayer and petition, with thanksgiving, present your requests to God. And the peace of God, which transcends all understanding, will guard your hearts and your minds in Christ Jesus."(NIV)

In this week's introduction, we saw a true warrior keep moving in the midst of extreme duress. In the process, he saved many of his fellow soldiers from certain death. In our battle, our job is to be Christs' tools on Earth. It is His ability to save the warriors among us, but it is our responsibility to keep moving alongside Him with trust, courage, and faith.

Warriors, it is our privilege to keep moving and fighting in the battles that our Risen Savior allows us to fight in. Put one foot in front of the other, and keep moving. When we do, the peace of God will flood our hearts, and make every step worth taking.

Thoughts in a Foxhole:

How does your David Moment fit into this "keep moving" thought process? In the space below, write down the instances when you may have gotten tired, and/or weary, and wanted to stop along your David Journey, but didn't. Thinking back to our story in the introduction, Robert's "keep moving" moments weren't saving the wounded, it was being shot while he was doing his job. Stripping it down further, it was the fear and pain associated with getting shot again, that was his true "keep moving" moment. So, figure out your "keep moving" moment, and then dissect it.

_____

_____

_____

_____

_____

_____

_____

_____

_____

_____

_____

LESSON THREE
VICTORY!

Yay! Ladies, we've made it! It has taken at least six weeks to get us through this study, but the end is here. Through many hours of Bible study, contemplation, and prayer, we have learned not only about our David Moment, but also through our David Moment. We've learned how to have courage, and how to relieve ourselves of worry and fear. We've learned about Satan's role in our David Moment. Then, we turned a corner, and started using God, the Great I Am, as our shield, and praying audaciously. We started really listening to God, and letting Him establish our steps. Finally, we have learned about the war, the battle, and our role as Warriors.

Today, we get to understand and celebrate our *victory*. We discussed how every David Moment, every core hurt, and every battle is unique. In the same way, every victory is exceptional and priceless. When Jesus won the war by dying on the cross and rising from the grave three days later, He created a victory meant especially for you. We are going to learn to identify that victory, and the victories in our lives, and in our David Moments.

Sometimes, the victories are obvious; yet other times, the victories have to be sought and understood. The following story is one of my favorite victory stories of all time. See if you can spot the victory.

Derek Redmond, a retired athlete from England, understands disappointment, but his story ends in the kind of victory only a loving God can put together. Derek was a promising runner in the 400 meter race in the Beijing Summer Olympics of 1992. He did well, but, halfway through the semi-final race, he felt searing pain in his leg, and fell to the ground. Seeing that his dream of the Olympics was coming to a close, he got up off of the ground, and decided to hobble to the finish line. After a few feet, he fell again, and with pain and hot tears stinging his face, he tried to figure out how to get up and keep moving. Just then, his father, Jim, barged through the security line. On the television screen I couldn't hear him, but I could see him yell at the guard, "That is my son!" He got on the race track, put his arms under his son's, and carried his son to the finish line.[9]

Many of you probably remember this story. Some of you may even remember seeing it happen on TV while watching the Olympics. Who won the gold medal? Can't remember? Neither do I. It wasn't Derek.

Derek may not have won the gold medal, but he certainly had a victory. Out of all the Olympic Games I have watched in my lifetime, it is this race, and this runner that I remember the most. It is the story of the victory of relationship. It is the story of the victory of tenacity, and it is the story of the victory of love.

Oh, sister, this is us! Our Father in Heaven is going to make sure you have a victory to celebrate. Just like Jim, nothing will stop your Heavenly Dad. He is the Alpha and the Omega, He is the Creator of Heaven and Earth, and He is the Lion of Judah. Security can't stop Him, Satan can't stop Him, and you can't even get in the way of Him loving you and fighting for you, and for your victory.

Let's look at some of the victories in the Bible, and learn to start seeing the victories in our lives, and in our David Moments.

The King David Connection:

Oh, ladies, I am so excited to share this last lesson with you. We are going to work together, and look at many victory stories in the Bible. Some victories are easily distinguished, while others are more difficult. Throughout this lesson, start to let your own victory story seep into your thoughts. This lesson is our celebration. Come celebrate with me!

Esther

Read Esther 7:1-8:8. Describe Esther's victory.

_____

_____

_____

_____

_____

_____

I love Esther's victory story. It is so dramatic. The bad guys lost and the good guys won. Hurrah!

Shadrach, Meshach, Abednego

Read Daniel 3:16-30. Describe Shadrach, Meshach, and Abednego's victory story.

_____

_____

_____

_____

_____

_____

Don't you just want to jump up and down, and cheer for the faith of these three men!

Ruth

Read Ruth 4:1-13. Describe Ruth's victory. This may require the knowledge of what happened to Ruth in chapters 1-3. If you already know Ruth's story, go ahead and answer the question. If you do not, take the time to read about Ruth, and the sacrifice she made to get to her victory. This was one courageous woman.

_____

_____

_____

_____

_____

_____

I appreciate Ruth's victory story because it is so real. This is a story you can imagine occurring today, yet her sacrifice and courage were remarkable, and something not seen often. I so appreciate that her daring actions of moving to a new land, taking care of her mother-in-law, and then practically asking a man to marry her, led her to being included in the lineage of King David and Jesus. Wow, what a victory!

Read 2 Kings 2:6-11. Describe Elijah's victory story.

_____

_____

_____

_____

_____

_____

Elijah was one of the few people to not die before going to heaven. What a dramatic exit from this world.

Anna the Prophetess

Read Luke 2:36-38. We don't know very much about this woman, Anna, but I love and respect her. In order to glean things from her, we have to think through what we know, and then apply those things to the culture of the day.

Her life was what many of us would characterize as disappointing. She was widowed at a very young age, without children, or the resources to provide for herself. She was allowed to live in the temple, which wouldn't have been allowed for just anyone, therefore, we know that she was respected. She prayed, fasted, and prophesied all the days of her life, never leaving the temple. She spent her life prophesying about the coming Messiah, before He was even born.

Describe Anna the Prophetess' victory story.

_____

_____

_____

_____

_____

I adore this sweet lady, and the grace which God gave her; Anna had the opportunity to see the birth of Jesus, and the honor of telling Jesus' parents that their child was the King.

Stephen

Read Acts 7:48-60. Describe Stephen's victory story. Some of the stories above have been obvious; this one is less so. I wish we could sit with a cup of coffee and compare notes. There are several ways in which you can consider his victory story, so read, contemplate, and write it down.

_____

_____

_____

_____

_____

Early followers of Jesus often had dramatic ends, yet that doesn't negate the power of their victory story. Stephen was filled to overflowing with the Holy Spirit, so much so that the heavens opened, and He was given a glimpse of what was to come, even before his death. Praise God!

Paul

Read 2 Timothy 4:1-8. This victory story is the most difficult to decipher. This is commonly considered one of the Apostle Paul's last days. The Bible does not give a specific account of Paul's death, but the manner of his death is not important. I will give you a hint; to find his victory story, look at his life.

_____

_____

_____

_____

_____

I believe that Paul's greatest victory lies in one word: legacy. Paul, being led by the Holy Spirit, wrote nearly half of the New Testament, thirteen books, in all. We have read some amazing victory stories, but one like Paul's is what I hope and pray for myself. I pray that I leave a legacy that reflects, glorifies, and proclaims the victory of Christ!

Ladies, we have read so much of David's story. There are three small victory stories: his victory against the giant, his victory against King Saul, and his victory against Absalom. These, however aren't his greatest victory. His greatest victory is forever being known as the man after God's own heart. How can a man who committed adultery, covered it up, and murdered to do so, be a man after God's own heart? The answer lies in his deep regret and repentance. David did a great deal wrong in his days, but when confronted by his sin, his repentance was real.

Sisters, when I leave this Earth, I want to leave like the runner from our introduction story. I don't want to look shiny, new, and beautiful. I want to hobble across the finish line, with my Heavenly Dad holding me up and saying, "Well done, good and faithful servant." This, I pray, will be my victory story.

What is yours? This is your time. Your David Moment is getting a makeover. What Satan put into place to trip you up, God is going to help you use as a step stool.

It is time to take that step. Your hurt can't get you down anymore. Your fear and worry are powerless. Your Shield, your Protector, your Creator, your Dad, and the Great I Am, is lifting your face, and reaching for your hand. Take it! Lay down your swords of bitterness, fear, vengeance, and anger. Pick up the sword of truth. It is through God's sword, through His power, through His mercy, and through His grace, that we will experience true and everlasting victory.

You are a Warrior, Sister. Now fight!

Thoughts in a Foxhole:

Reflecting on your David Moment, what do you feel are victories you have already experienced? Write down your list.

Week Six
Battle Plan

Consult with the General

Talk to your Heavenly Dad, and ask Him to guide you to your victory story. What ultimate victory story do you want your life to represent? Write down what God says.

_____

_____

_____

_____

_____

_____

_____

_____

_____

_____

_____

_____

_____

_____

Your Tactical Plan

What do you do from here? This is the space where we start to give your David Moment its makeover. How are you being led by God to transform your moment into a victory? Be specific. What does the Warrior within you want to do, to make your David Moment victorious?

_____

_____

_____

_____

_____

_____

_____

_____

_____

_____

_____

_____

WEEK SIX REVIEW

You did it! Congratulations! Do you feel transformed? As I said in the conclusion, you will never be the same. What once was a difficulty that Satan exploited, our living God has turned into a stepping stool. You are a Warrior capable of changing the world through the power of God.

This week's lessons helped you see the power and importance in forgiveness, the importance of keeping on the move, and it introduced you to your victory story. Each chapter in this study built on the previous chapters. You were not ready for week six during weeks one through five, but here you are.

You are a Warrior, and a precious member of God's vast army. I love you, my sister Warrior.

This week's Discussion Questions:

1. Have you had a forgiveness story that led you to healing? Share if you can.

2. How can forgiveness make you a stronger Warrior?

3. How do you feel when you have wronged someone? Are you quick to try to rid yourself of the feelings, or do you allow them to stay?

4. How has your David Moment included painful moments along the way?

5. How did you feel when painful moments did not go away, yet you still kept moving?

6. What victories have you experienced with your David Moment?

7. What would you like your ultimate victory to look like?

8. Do you feel like a Warrior? What do you feel led to do that you didn't before you began this study?

CONCLUSION

Charge!

Oh, my sweet sisters in Christ, can you see me jumping up and down in my study? I feel like I can see you cuddled on the couch, or seated at your kitchen table reading these words. I am so proud of you. When we started this study, I told you we would learn together. As I sit writing this, it was eighteen months ago that our family's "Chicago" happened. I was that wilting flower sitting in my bedroom, completely empty. When God presented this idea to me, I couldn't imagine being the person I am now. Early on, I had to come to terms with whether or not I was ready to write this study, and I prayed to Jesus that I was ready to type, but He would have to write. He has been with me every step of the way, and with every word. Every time I would finish a chapter, I would be inundated with opportunities to learn that lesson. I cannot tell you the work my Heavenly Dad has done in and through me throughout the last eighteen months.

I have enough faith in my Savior that I can say, without a doubt, that He has done the same for you. Whether you understand it or not, you are different than the person who began this study. From the first word typed, God has led me to an obscure story in the Bible. I wasn't sure where it would go or why it would be in the study, but now I do.

This story is found in Ezekiel 37:1-10:

> The hand of the Lord was on me, and he brought me out by the Spirit of the Lord and set me in the middle of a valley; it was full of bones. He led me back and forth among them, and I saw a great many bones on the floor of the valley, bones that were very dry. He asked me, "Son of man, can these bones live?"
>
> I said, "Sovereign Lord, you alone know."
>
> Then he said to me, "Prophesy to these bones and say to them, 'Dry bones, hear the word of the Lord! This is what the Sovereign Lord says to these bones: I

will make breath enter you, and you will come to life. I will attach tendons to you and make flesh come upon you and cover you with skin; I will put breath in you, and you will come to life. Then you will know that I am the Lord.'"

So I prophesied as I was commanded. And as I was prophesying, there was a noise, a rattling sound, and the bones came together, bone to bone. I looked, and tendons and flesh appeared on them and skin covered them, but there was no breath in them.

Then he said to me, "Prophesy to the breath; prophesy, son of man, and say to it, 'This is what the Sovereign Lord says: Come, breath, from the four winds and breathe into these slain, that they may live.'" So I prophesied as he commanded me, and breath entered them; they came to life and stood up on their feet—a vast army. (NIV)

Sisters, WE are His army! We are His warriors! You are ready. You are no longer dry bones; you are the living, breathing, and very much loved, army of God!

I love you, dear friends and sisters.

LEADER'S GUIDE

WELCOME LETTER

I am so excited that you have chosen to lead this Bible study. Thank you for your trust.

It was my goal in preparing this, for it to be available for three different Bible study viewers: one, that a person could pull it off of the shelf, and complete it alone as part of their quiet time at home; two, that a small group could choose it and work through it together; and, three, that a larger group could use a more formal approach with a leader giving a small presentation before the group discussion. I'll go through each format.

A single person: I can't tell you how many Bible studies I've completed in just this way. As we all do, I have a few favorite Bible teachers, and I hate to miss one of their new studies, so I go to my local Bible bookstore, and go through it on my own. If this is you, have fun! Feel free to read through this leader's guide, you might get additional information, and/or glean important details.

Small group: The church I've been a part of is smaller in size. We have a vibrant women's ministry, yet that only consists of fifteen ladies. When we work through a study, we need to have weekly homework and discussion questions. If you are the leader of a small women's study, here is an idea for formatting this study for your group, which will take approximately one and a half hours to complete:

Welcome/Fellowship
Prayer
Review Battle plan
Weekly review questions
Read the next week's introduction
Prayer requests/prayer

Large group/ group with leader presentation: If you are planning on a small presentation before each lesson, I commend you; it takes more study and preparation to do this. I will give you an idea of the topics to cover in your presentation and then leave it to you to fill in with your personal stories and background. Here is an idea for the format (very similar to above), that will take you approximately two hours to complete:

Welcome/Fellowship
Prayer
Presentation by leader
Divide into smaller groups, if needed
Review battle plan
Weekly review questions
Read the next week's introduction
Prayer requests/prayer

Again, thank you for choosing this study to help you go deeper into the Bible. I'm excited to get started with you, and to initiate more Warriors into the battle.

In His love,
Heather

INTRODUCTION MEETING THOUGHTS

Dear Leader,

This first meeting of the group is a good opportunity to explain the format of the study, how the study is going to work, and how to go about completing the homework. I suggest that you keep the format similar to the format you will use for all presentations with one difference; during the group discussion time, complete the first lesson. So, your format for this meeting will look like this:

Welcome/Fellowship

Prayer

Read Week One introduction

Presentation by leader

Divide into smaller groups, if needed

Complete week one, lesson one

Prayer requests/prayer

As you are the group leader, I am going to ask that you are vulnerable in sharing your story. Your honesty and willingness to share who you are and your own journey to becoming a Warrior, may make it easier for others to fully participate. In a group such as this, we all have the opportunity to learn from each other. Please impress upon them that you are sharing so that they, too, will share.

When you pass the baton to the small group leaders (SGLs), they will be in charge of the discussion. There is an art to effectively leading discussions in a group such as this. Train your SGLs to impress upon their group the importance of everyone sharing. In order to do this, everyone needs to prayerfully plan to share their story, be prepared to listen, and be absolutely quiet about others' stories outside their group. There will always be those who are more prone to talk, and those who are more prone to stay quiet. Explain ahead of time that you understand both situations, and that you hope all will allow the others to learn from their story; therefore all are prepared to be called on and participate. There may be times when the SGLs need to gently cut off a "talker" and ask what a "non-talker" thinks. This can feel awkward, but if you wait for a slight pause in what the person is saying, it can be less so. Conversations in small groups easily get off track; in a similar way as above, the SGLs should lovingly keep the conversation on track.

In the first meeting, the SGLs will need to explain the Battle Plan that will be found at the end of each week. Some people who will attend this study will have never had alone time with God, listening to His words. It is important to explain the process and how they can be comfortable with the answers they hear. I always tell people to get to a comfortable, quiet place, where they will experience no interruptions. They should start out by praising Him, praying (communicating) to God, petitioning (requesting) his help, answers, and/or presence. Then they will wait on the Lord. He will answer every one of us. Once they hear the answer, they need to test the words heard against Scripture. Are they accurate and biblical? If the person is unclear, they need to ask a mature Christian friend to help them determine their next move biblically.

Finally, it is important during this first meeting that either you, or the SGLs ask the participants to be determined in completing the homework. This is a topical Bible study, and if they skip a lesson, they will miss an important piece of the "becoming a Warrior" puzzle. There are three lessons per week. Most studies have five days of homework. You will find that the time it takes to complete the three lessons from our study, will be similar to the time it would take participants to complete the five lessons in other studies. This makes the time to complete each lesson in the Warrior slightly longer than if we divided it into five days, but the participants can divide it themselves as they see fit. Each week will require approximately 1- 1 1/2 hours of work. The homework that needs to be completed before each meeting is as follows:

> The three weekly lessons
> The week's Battle Plan

The weekly review should be looked at, but it isn't necessary to complete before the meeting.

I'm thrilled to join you as you lead this study.
In His love,
Heather

INTRODUCTION WEEK AGENDA/NOTES

Welcome/Fellowship
Prayer
Read week one introduction
Presentation by leader

- Read Psalm 3 to the group
- Explain who wrote Psalm 3 and the setting
  The author of Psalm 3 is King David.
  The setting of Psalm 3 is explained, in detail, in 2 Samuel 15-18
- Explain how this study follows Psalm 3. Here are my thoughts, but feel free to use your own words.
  This study will follow Psalm 3. We will join King David as his heart is broken and his faith is wobbly. We will start by finding our own event, time, or season that emulates King David's broken heart, and travel with him as he decides to trust in God. Finally, we will share in his victory. King David ultimately (and while people were still hunting him) proclaimed his faith in the power of God and forgiveness for those people hunting him. We will learn to do the same through the next six weeks of lessons. By the end of this study it is my prayer that you, like King David, will use this difficult time in your life to find the Warrior inside of you who is willing and able to fight for their faith and the faith of those they love. You will become a Warrior for the Creator of the Universe.
- Share your David Moment (as explained in week one lesson one).
  The goal for this lesson is for each participant to identify their David Moment. You sharing yours will help them start to identify theirs, and it will also set a good example of the vulnerability they need to develop for this study as a whole.

Divide into smaller groups

- The SGLs will go through and complete the first lesson with their group.
- Prayer requests/prayer

WEEK ONE
AGENDA/NOTES

Welcome/Fellowship
Prayer
Presentation by leader

- We mention throughout the study that "the war is won." Clarify for your group what "the war" is. I will give you the words from the study below, but please feel free to word this differently.

  > You might not realize it but there is a war being waged all around us. It started the second Satan wanted to be considered equal to our Father in Heaven. Ever since that moment, Satan has been fighting for influence in this world and in your heart. It is a war between good and evil but also so much more. Whether or not you choose to fight you are a warrior in the greatest war ever fought. The best news of all is that the second Jesus took a breath in His burial tomb, the war itself was won, but there are still battles to fight and that is where you come in.

- Review the six core hurts and their definitions

  1. Fear
  2. Anxiety/Worry
  3. Disappointment
  4. Loss
  5. Pain (physical, emotional or spiritual)
  6. Temptation

- Consider giving an example of your choice for the 6 core hurts from the Bible. For example, the woman at the well from John 4.

- o Discuss how her core hurt could have been a number of different hurts but that in your opinion her core hurt was _____. Explain that it was through the grace of God that that core hurt disappeared.
- Review the four ways Satan can influence us. Explain each:

  1. No influence – review how Satan can be blamed for too much – given too much credit.
  2. Demonic influence
  3. Oppression
  4. Possession – Explain how this cannot happen to the children of God.

- Finish your presentation with a personal experience that involved Demonic Influence or Oppression.

Divide into smaller groups, if needed:

- Go over battle plan for week one
- Weekly review questions for week one
- Read week two's introduction

Prayer requests/prayer

WEEK TWO
AGENDA/NOTES

Welcome/Fellowship
Prayer
Presentation by leader

- Go over the definitions and differences between worry, anxiety, and fear. Use biblical and personal examples to bring clarification to these often confused details

  <u>Worry</u> is a choice we make. It is a pattern we choose to indulge. Worry is a prolonged state of anxiety.

  <u>Anxiety</u> is a physiological response designed to protect us from the anticipation of the possibility of a threat.

  <u>Fear</u> is our response to an immediate (real or perceived) threat.

- Anxiety and fear are God-given protections against threats. Yet prolonged anxiety, worry, along with fear need to be given to God so that we are able to go into battle with the peace, faith, and trust God intended. Give an example in your life how you gave up worry and or fear to trust Jesus.

- Go through the difference between brave and courage.

  <u>Brave</u> is a character trait with which we are born.

  <u>Courage</u> is being afraid but having faith anyway. Courage is having faith in God beyond the fear.

- Give an example of courage found in the Bible. Remember, while worry and fear are something we need to give- to God, courage is a gift from God. There are many examples in the Bible of people who were initially afraid of the path in front of them yet trusted God and went forward with courage.

Divide into smaller groups, if needed:

- Go over battle plan for week two
- Weekly review questions for week two
- Read week three's introduction

Prayer requests/prayer

WEEK THREE
AGENDA/NOTES

Welcome/Fellowship
Prayer
Presentation by leader

- The following is an exercise with the verses from Psalms that we are centering on this week: Go through the exercise at the beginning of week three lesson 2's King David Connection. Ask the participants to close their eyes while you slowly read Psalm 3: 3-4 out loud. Ask them to choose one thing that stood out for them. Ask them if they can picture the one thing that stood out for them helping King David? Finally, ask them to apply the thing that helped King David in their own life.
- Review the four shields and read the Bible verse that goes with each.

  1. Faith – Ephesians 6:16. Share your daily flaming arrows you deal with
  2. Protection – Deuteronomy.
  3. Refuge – Proverbs 30:5.
  4. Salvation – 2 Samuel 22:36. Make the distinction that this kind of salvation was for David's rescue, safety and victory in battle. Briefly share your thoughts on what King David needed salvation from (there are many – both physical and spiritual) and then some daily things we all battle and need salvation from.

- Explain, in your own words, what it means for God to be the Great I Am. Explain it in the context of God living in the past, present and the future. We live in a linier world, but God does not.
- Briefly describe the scene from Joshua 10:7-14. Explain that Joshua refused to limit God and then ask the participants if they have inadvertently limited God (I know I have). Share an audacious prayer you have prayed since doing this lesson. Challenge them to do the same.

Divide into smaller groups, if needed:

- Go over battle plan for week three
- Weekly review questions for week three
- Read week four's introduction

Prayer requests/prayer

WEEK FOUR
AGENDA/NOTES

Welcome/Fellowship
Prayer
Presentation by leader

- Share a story about when you heard and listened to God. Was it more like the story of Elijah or David?
- Read Proverbs 16:9
- Through the story you gave above, how did you see God establishing your steps? Give the definition you found for establishes and directs.
- Compare and contrast the plans us humans hearts make with how the Lord establishes our steps.
- Share what we feel like when we are spiritually lost (get ideas from the Isaiah 41:10 deconstruction exercise in lesson 2) and God's remedy for it found in the same verse.
- Review the four different kinds of "*suddenlys*".

  1. Opportunities to see a miracle
  2. Displays the powerful presence of God
  3. Provide Important information
  4. Give us protection in battle

- Share a story where a *suddenly* helped you with one or more of the above and how it helped you become a better warrior in God's army.

Divide into smaller groups, if needed:

- Go over battle plan for week four
- Weekly review questions for week four
- Read week five's introduction

Prayer requests/prayer

WEEK FIVE
AGENDA/NOTES

Welcome/Fellowship
Prayer
Presentation by leader

- Make sure that the participants realize there are three different levels of warfare.

  The war
  The battle
  The soldier

- Give your testimony. Explain how each story, like yours, is a battle won and a result of the war that is already won.
- The war – read each verse and explain why it is the beginning/present/future of the war. Set the stage for the last verse (Romans 6:23 is the pinnacle verse for our faith.

  Beginning – Isaiah 14:12-15
  Present - 2 Corinthians 4:1-6
  Future - Romans 6:8-11 and 23

- Go over the two aspects of the battle we are all involved in.

  Satan wants to destroy God's influence in our life
  Satan wants to destroy God's influence in other's life through us – this, my friends, is the Great Commission.

- Ask them, what do Rahab, Jael, Hannah, Lois, Eunice, and YOU have in common? We are all Warriors in God's army. If you have the chance to ask ahead of time, get permission to quickly go through stories of a couple people in your audience on how they are warriors. For example:

Jan helped with VBS this summer
Carol talked about Jesus to a friend last week
Madison volunteered with her church in a soup kitchen last week
How many of you have ever prayed for a friend's salvation? Congratulations you are a Warrior in God's army.

Divide into smaller groups, if needed:

- Go over battle plan for week five
- Weekly review questions for week five
- Read week six's introduction

Prayer requests/prayer

WEEK SIX
AGENDA/NOTES

Welcome/Fellowship

Prayer

Presentation by leader (I have gone into much more detail on your presentation here. Please feel free to use as much or as little as you'd like)

- Ladies we are at the end of our Warrior training. We have learned:

  What we are fighting
  We have gained a Warrior mentality
  We have learned that God is our powerful protector
  We have gone through Spiritual Boot camp
  And we have learned about the three levels of warfare.
  We have a little bit more to learn and then we get our marching orders

- What can we learn from Warrior women of the Bible?
  - Deborah was a shrewd military leader who was greatly out numbered. She tricked the enemy into driving their iron wheeled chariots into a marshy field getting them stuck. Then the archers of Israel picked them off one by one
  - Jael sent a tent peg through her enemy's head when he went to sleep
  - Judith cut off the head of the enemy general and mounted it so that the enemy could see, thus panicking the troops so that they were easy prey for the Israelites
  - Esther - courage - risked her life to save her people
  - Ruth – Selflessness
  - Rahab was a spy
  - The hunched over woman from Luke dealt with an infirmity for 18 years but kept faith and kept seeking God.

- o Mary mother of Jesus had faith which she showed over and over – trust with getting pregnant and then – watching son get murdered

Forgiveness

- Every one of these ladies had to have a forgiving heart. UN-forgiveness clouds the heart and makes our witness infinitely more difficult.
- Let's look at Romans 5:3-4. Rejoice in our sufferings? We know why, but How? – through forgiveness. Ephesians 4:31-32
  - o Romans 5:3-4: Not only that, but we rejoice in our sufferings, knowing that suffering produces endurance, [4] and endurance produces character, and character produces hope
  - o Ephesians 4:31-32: Get rid of all bitterness, rage and anger, brawling and slander, along with every form of malice. [32]Be kind and compassionate to one another, forgiving each other, just as in Christ God forgave you.
- Have you experienced the hope and that comes through forgiveness?
- David not only forgives his persecutors – while they are still hunting him – he asks God to bless them. Think about a person you need to forgive…have you asked God to bless them?
- Your plan on forgiveness - just do it!

Keep Moving

- There is obedience in moving forward despite _____. Pain, discouragement, wobbly faith…
- What are you moving forward through?
- Can moving forward help others? Think about Joab. He forced David to keep moving after the death of his son. How did David's movement help others?
- In the study it says that occasionally God makes some mountains unmovable. We need to praise Him for who He is not what He does. Thinking about your DM, why do you praise God?

Divide into smaller groups, if needed:

- Go over battle plan for week six
- Weekly review questions for week six
- Read Charge! (after the last lesson)

Prayer requests shared in small group

Go back to full group:

- What is your victory story?
- Option: Give out Warrior Woman metals.

Full group prayer

Bibliography

Week One

1. "Alan Fowler." 26 Mar. 2017.

Week Two

1. Adapted story from historical information: "Kroll, Chana. *Irena Sendler Rescuer of the Children of Warsaw.*
2. "TOP 8 QUOTES BY IRENA SENDLER." *A-Z Quotes*, www.azquotes.com/author/30375-Irena_Sendler.
3. Simpson, Amy. *Anxiety: Choosing Faith in a World of Worry.*
4. Benson. "Biblehub." *2 Samuel 15 Benson Commentary*, biblehub.com/commentaries/benson/2_samuel/15.htm.
5. Adapted story from historical information: "Writer, Ron Jackson Staff. "Surviving the Dust Bowl." *NDepth: Surviving the Dust Bowl Storms of the 1930's | Newsok.com*, ndepth.newsok.com/dustbowl.
6. Adapted story from historical information:"116th Infantry." *116th Infantry History*, 29thdivisionassociation. com/116th%20Infantry%20history.html.
7. "KB." 12 May 2017.

Week Three

1. "Lesson 5: The Shield of Faith." *Free Bible Study Guides*, United Church of God, an International Association, www.freebiblestudyguides.org/bible-teachings/armor-of-god-shield-of-faith.htm.
2. Shirer, Priscilla. "Who's Your Daddy?" *YouTube*, YouTube, www.youtube.com/.

Week Four

1. Davis, Jon. "Why Are Military Boot Camps Are So Intense?" *Slate Magazine*, 5 Mar. 2013, www.slate.com/ blogs/quora/2013/03/05/why_is_boot_camp_so_intense.html.
2. Trottman, Jacki. "Be Still and Know That I Am God – The Meaning of Be Still will Surprise You." *The Guided Life*, 11 May 2017, guidedchristianmeditation.com/181/meditation/ be-still-and-know-that-i-am-god-the-meaning-of-be-still-will-surprise-you/.

3. George. "Managing Your 50,000 Daily Thoughts." *Sentient Developments*, 19 Mar. 2007, www.sentientdevelopments.com/2007/03/managing-your-50000-daily-thoughts.html.

4. "Joshua Hurley" May 2017

Week Five

1. Lomong, Lopez, and Mark A. Tabb. *Running for My Life: One Lost Boy's Journey from the Killing Fields of Sudan to the Olympic Games*. Nelson Books, an Imprint of Thomas Nelson, 2016.

2. Member of the Combined Joint Special Operations Air Component, Anonymous. 1 June 2017.

Week Six

1. Kemp, Thomas Jay. "Angela Cavallo Saves Her Son's Life with Her Supermom Strength."*GenealogyBank Blog*, 10 May 2013, blog.genealogybank.com/angela-cavallo-saves-her-sons-life-with-her-supermom-strength.html.

2. Reporter, Daily Mail. "Heroic Father Punches out Alligator to Save His Son from the Reptile's Jaws." *Daily Mail Online*, Associated Newspapers, 21 Apr. 2013, www.dailymail.co.uk/news/article-2312598/Heroic-father-punches-alligator-save-son-reptiles-jaws.html.

3. Vlogger. "Man Lifts Crashed Helo to Save Vet." *Military.com*, Vlogger, 7 July 2011, www.military.com/video/aircraft/helicopters/man-lifts-crashed-helo-to-save-vet/1042307532001.

4. Vant, Rebecca: www.listverse.com

5. Fowler, Heather, and Anonymous, "Michelle." "Forgiveness Story." 31 Jan. 2018.

6. Fowler, Heather, and Anonymous, "Graceli Veson." "Forgiveness story." 12 Sept. 2017

7. ten Boom, Corrie. "Guideposts Classics: Corrie Ten Boom on Forgiveness." *Guideposts*, 27 June 2017, www.guideposts.org/better-living/positive-living/guideposts-classics-corrie-ten-boom-on-forgiveness.

8. dapted Story Using Historical Information: *ROBERT R. INGRAM*, fightingpatriot.com/robert%20r%20ingram.html.

9. User, Super. "Derek Redmond-a Great Father-Son Story." *NPO*, www.nationalparentsorganization.org/blog/722-derek-redmond-a-grea.

NOTES

Printed in the United States
By Bookmasters